Information Technology Law in Hong Kong

Information Technology Law in Hong Kong

Yun Zhao

This book was originally published as a monograph in the International Encyclopaedia of Laws/Privacy and Technology Law.

Founding Editor: Roger Blanpain
General Editor: Frank Hendrickx
Volume Editors: Jos Dumortier, Pieter Gryffroy, Ruben Roex & Yung Shin Van Der Sype

Wolters Kluwer

Published by:
Kluwer Law International B.V.
PO Box 316
2400 AH Alphen aan den Rijn
The Netherlands
E-mail: lrs-sales@wolterskluwer.com
Website: www.wolterskluwer.com/en/solutions/kluwerlawinternational

Sold and distributed by:
Wolters Kluwer Legal & Regulatory U.S.
920 Links Avenue
Landisville, PA 17538
United States of America
E-mail: customer.service@wolterskluwer.com

ISBN 978-94-035-2276-0

e-Book: ISBN 978-94-035-2496-2
web-PDF: ISBN 978-94-035-2506-8

The Author

Yun Zhao, PhD (Erasmus University Rotterdam), LLM (Leiden University), LLM & LLB (the China University of Political Science and Law), is Henry Cheng Professor in International Law and Head of the Department of Law at the University of Hong Kong. He is currently a Representative of the Regional Office for Asia and the Pacific of the Hague Conference on Private International Law and also Chair Professor at Xiamen University. He is listed as an arbitrator in several international arbitration commissions. He is also the founding Council Member of the Hong Kong Internet Forum, a Member of the International Institute of Space Law in Paris, Member of the Asia Pacific Law Association and Beijing International Law Society. He sits on the editorial teams of several Social Sciences Citation Index journals, including *Hong Kong Law Journal* (as China Law editor) and *the Journal of East Asia and International Law* (as Executive Editor). He is the winner of Prof. Dr I.H.Ph. Diederiks-Verschoor Award 2006, awarded by the International Institute of Space Law in France, the first winner of the Isa Diederiks-Verschoor Prize in the Netherlands, and also the first winner of the SATA Prize, awarded by the Foundation of Development of International Law in Asia. He has published widely on various topics, including particularly dispute resolution and space law. His publications include: *Dispute Resolution in Electronic Commerce* (Martinus Nijhoff, 2005); *Liberalization of Electronic Commerce and Law* (Peking University Press, 2005); *Space Commercialization and the Development of Space Law* (Intellectual Property Press, 2008); *Mediation Practice and Skills* (Tsinghua University Press, 2011); *National Space Legislation in China: An Overview of the Current Situation and Outlook for the Future* (Brill, 2015).

The Author

Table of Contents

The Author 3

List of Abbreviations 13

Preface 17

General Introduction 19

Chapter 1. General Background of the Region 19

Chapter 2. Telecommunications Infrastructure 23

Chapter 3. The Information and Communications Technology Market 27

Chapter 4. e-Commerce: Facts and Figures 31

§1. Development of Internet-Based e-Commerce 31

§2. Types of e-Commerce 31

§3. Development of e-Commerce via Mobile Devices 32

§4. Internet Banking and Business 32

§5. e-Commerce Providers 33

§6. Overview 34

Chapter 5. e-Government Initiatives 35

§1. Basic Understanding 35

§2. Ongoing Efforts 36

§3. 'Digital 21' and Other Policy Initiatives 38

§4. A Solid and Flexible Internal Government Infrastructure and Support 40

Part I. Regulation of the ICT Market 41

Chapter 1. Regulatory Framework of the Telecommunications Sector 41

§1. Regulatory Background 41

§2. Legal Framework 42

§3. Licensing Regimes 43

§4. Liberalization of the Telecommunications Sector 44

Chapter 2. Regulation of Competition in the ICT Market 47

§1. General Background 47

§2. Governmental Arrangements 48

§3. Regulation on Discounts to Published Tariffs 49

§4. Ongoing Process 49

Chapter 3. Regulation of Cryptography and Other Dual-Use Goods 51

§1. General Background 51

§2. Regulations in Hong Kong 52

Chapter 4. Legal Status of Standardization 54

Chapter 5. Legal Status of Out-of-Court Dispute Settlement in the ICT Sector 56

§1. Background 56

§2. Domain Name Dispute Resolution 56

§3. HKDNR Domain Name Dispute Resolution Policy 58

§4. Rules of Procedure 59

§5. Electronic Transaction Arbitration Rules 60

§6. Electronic Business Related Arbitration and Mediation 62

Part II. Protection of Intellectual Property in the ICT Sector 63

Chapter 1. Application of Copyright in the Area of ICT 63

§1. General Introduction 63

§2. Copyright and Its Application Regarding the Internet 63

§3. Moral Rights 65

§4. Primary Infringement 66

§5. Secondary Infringement 67

§6. Infringement on the Internet 67

§7. Copyright (Amendment) Ordinance 68

Chapter 2. Legal Protection of Software 70

Chapter 3. Legal Protection of Databases 73

Chapter 4. Legal Protection of Computer Chips 74

Chapter 5. Other Intellectual Property Rights in the ICT Sector 75

§1. Trademark Protection 75

§2. Patent Infringement 76

§3. Registered Design Rights 78

§4. Trade Secret 79

Chapter 6. Internet Domain Name Registration 80

§1. General Introduction 80

§2. Registration in Hong Kong 80

§3. Registration Rules 81

§4. Combating Cybersquatting 83

Part III. ICT Contracts 85

Chapter 1. Hardware Contracts 85

Chapter 2. Software Contracts 87

Chapter 3. Turnkey Contracts 89

Chapter 4. Distribution Agreements 91

Chapter 5. Maintenance Contracts 93

Chapter 6. Facilities Management 95

Chapter 7. Network Services 96

Chapter 8. Government Contracts 97

Part IV. Electronic Transactions 99

Chapter 1. Legal Status of Electronic Transactions 99

§1. Regulatory Framework for Electronic Transactions 99

§2. Application Scope of the ETO 100

§3. The Requirement of 'Writing' 101

§4. Formation of an Electronic Contract 102

§5. Implied Terms: The SGO and the SSITO 104

§6. The Control of Exemption Clauses Ordinance 105

§7. Bills Committee on Import and Export (Electronic Transactions) Bill 2001 105

§8. Jurisdiction and Choice of Law 106

Chapter 2. Regulation of Electronic Signatures and Certification Services 108

§1. Background 108

§2. Electronic Signature and Digital Signature 109

§3. Public Key Infrastructure 111

§4. Certification Services 111

§5. Subscriber Agreement for e-Cert 114

Chapter 3. Legal Aspects of Electronic Banking 116

§1. Background 116

§2. Authorization of e-Banks 117

§3. Management and Assessment of Security Aspects of Transactional e-Banking Services 119

§4. New Electronic Payment Systems 120

Chapter 4. Protection of Users of Electronic Services 122

Part V. Non-contractual Liability 125

Chapter 1. Negligence 125

§1. General Introduction 125

§2. Liability for Negligence 125

§3. Negligent Misstatements 126

Chapter 2. Liability of Network Operators 127

Chapter 3. Liability of Service Providers 128

§1. Regulations on ISPs 128

§2. Liability of ISPs 128

§3. Liability of ISPs in Case of Defamation 129

§4. Liability of ISPs in Case of Obscene and Indecent Articles 130

Chapter 4. Product Liability 133

Part VI. Privacy Protection 135

Chapter 1. Regulation of Personal Data Processing 135

§1. Personal Data (Privacy) Ordinance 135

§2. The Privacy Commissioner for Personal Data 136

§3. Data User Returns and Register of Data Users 138

§4. Access to and Correction of Personal Data 139

§5. Matching Procedures and Transfer of Information 139

§6. Transparency of the Policy on Personal Data Privacy 141

§7. Complaint Handling Policy 142

Chapter 2. Protection of Telecommunications Privacy 144

Part VII. Computer-Related Crime 145

Chapter 1. General Legal Development 145

Chapter 2. Application of Substantive Criminal Law in the Area of ICT 147

§1. Obscene and Indecent Content 147

§2. Sedition 150

§3. Sex Discrimination 151

§4. Disability Discrimination 151

§5. Family Status Discrimination 152

§6. Race Discrimination 153

§7. Internet Gambling 154

§8. Criminal Liability for Infringement of Copyright and Other Intellectual Property Rights 155

§9. Interception of Communications 156

§10. Offences Concerning Personal Data 158

§11. Telecommunications Offences (Transmission of Information) 158

Chapter 3. Application of Criminal Procedural Law in the Area of ICT 160

Chapter 4. Conclusions 163

Selected Bibliography 165

Index 167

Table of Contents

List of Abbreviations

ADNDRC	Asian Domain Name Dispute Resolution Centre
ASP	Application Services Provider
B2B	Business-to-Business
B2C	Business-to-Consumer
B2G	Business-to-Government
CA	Certification Authority
CIG	Central Internet Gateway
CTB	Communications and Technology Branch
DNDRP	Domain Name Dispute Resolution Policy
eBRAM	Electronic Business Related Arbitration and Mediation
EDI	Electronic Data Interchange
ESD	Electronic Service Delivery
ETO	Electronic Transactions Ordinance
ETS	External Telecommunications Services
FAQ	Frequently Asked Question
FCL	Fixed Carrier Licence
FTNS	Fixed Telecommunications Network Service
FTTB	Fibre-To-The-Building
FTTH	Fibre-To-The-Home
GDP	Gross Domestic Product
GLD	Government Logistics Department
gTLD	Generic Top-Level Domain
GSM	Global System for Mobile Communications
HKDNR	Hong Kong Domain Name Registration Company Limited
HKIAC	Hong Kong International Arbitration Centre
HKIRC	Hong Kong Internet Registration Corporation Limited
HKISPA	Hong Kong Internet Service Providers Association
HKMA	Hong Kong Monetary Authority
HKPost	Hong Kong Post Office
HKSA	Hong Kong Society of Accountants

List of Abbreviations

HKSAR	Hong Kong Special Administrative Region
HKTC	Hong Kong Telephone Company
IBM	International Business Machines
ICAC	Independent Commission Against Corruption
ICANN	Internet Corporation for Assigned Names and Numbers
ICP	Internet Content Provider
ICT	Information Communication and Technology
IIAC	Information Infrastructure Advisory Committee
IMSN	International Marketing Supervision Network
IP	Internet Protocol
ISO	International Standards Organization
ISP	Internet Service Provider
IT	Information Technology
ITBB	Information Technology and Broadcasting Bureau
ITC	Innovation and Technology Commission
ITSD	Information Technology Services Department
ITU	International Telecommunications Union
JUCC	Joint Universities Computer Centre
LAN	Local Area Network
LMDS	Local Multipoint Distribution System
MVNO	Mobile Virtual Network Operator
OAT	Obscene Articles Tribunal
OECD	Organisation for Economic Co-operation and Development
OFTA	Office of the Telecommunications Authority
PC	Personal Computer
PCO	Privacy Commissioner's Office
PDA	Personal Digital Assistant
PIN	Personal Identification Number
PKI	Public Key Infrastructure
PRC	People's Republic of China
PSIB	Product Standards Information Bureau
SBO	Services-Based Operator
SCL	Standards and Calibration Laboratory
SGO	Sale of Goods Ordinance
SI	International System
SLD	Second-Level Domain
SME	Small and Medium-Sized Enterprise
SSITO	Supply of Services (Implied Terms) Ordinance
TA	Telecommunications Authority

TLD	Top-Level Domain
UCL	Unified Carrier Licence
UDRP	Uniform Domain Name Dispute Resolution Policy
UNCITRAL	United Nations Commission on International Trade Law
WLAN	Wireless Local Area Networks
WTO	World Trade Organization

List of Abbreviations

Preface

A decade after the turn of the millennium, an ever-increasing proportion of the population is electronically linked through global information networks. More importantly, such networks are commercially exploited, with the term 'e-commerce' being popularly recognized. Around the world, the introduction of e-commerce is bringing about profound changes in societies, economies and legal systems, impacting the way we live, learn, interact socially, do business and govern ourselves.

This monograph provides basic guidance to cyber law in Hong Kong. It shows in detail how both the institutional and regulatory frameworks in Hong Kong implement e-commerce. These frameworks channel technology and guide the legal implementation of the actual connections in Hong Kong.

The monograph tries to offer a complete overview of the legal rules on regulating e-commerce in Hong Kong. The academic and government communities in Hong Kong are more actively considering the implications of the accelerated process of global technological integration for public policymaking. Against this background, I try to provide a complete examination of existing statutes and ordinances, which can have implications for e-commerce. I also take into account further developments in this field and new and proposed rules and regulations.

General Introduction

Chapter 1. General Background of the Region

1. Often claimed as the best example of 'East meets West', Hong Kong is indeed a city of marked contrasts. Historically, Hong Kong has served as Mainland China's window to the world for more than a century and a half since the Chinese government was forced to cede Hong Kong to the British after the Opium Wars in 1841. Since then, the British government has transplanted English lifestyle rules to Hong Kong. It quickly became a base for opium export into China, as well as for the sale of tea, porcelain, and other Chinese goods to Europe. The establishment of the Hong Kong Special Administration Region under the People's Republic of China (PRC) in 1997 opened a new page for this oriental pearl.

2. Hong Kong has one of the world's most dramatic harbours, with breathtaking views everywhere. It covers an area of 1,100 square kilometres with a population of more than 7 million and, thus, is a densely populated region. Nearly 200 uninhabited islands lie within Hong Kong waters in the South China Sea, while the Kowloon neighbourhood of Kwun Tong is the most densely populated area among the District Council districts. 92% of the population as of 2016 is Chinese. Chinese and English are the official languages. Cantonese is widely used as a Chinese dialect. Conversing with neighbouring communities in Chinese can bridge the language gap between China and the rest of the world. Hong Kong's openness to foreigners and different cultures allows the merging of the best of both technology and knowledge.

3. Nearly three-quarters of Hong Kong is undeveloped, and most lies within the Country Parks System. Commerce and trade are the lifeblood of Hong Kong, and the value of both imports and exports exceeds the Gross National Product of Hong Kong.

4. Toys and movies are two industries in which Hong Kong has enjoyed past success. Hong Kong toy companies have in fact become virtual manufacturers that can prototype, produce and distribute toys from sub-contracted factories and warehouses in Mainland China, keeping capital infrastructure low and supply chains flexible. Hong Kong's film industry, taking the style of amusement from Hollywood films, has achieved worldwide recognition.[1]

5. Financial services, tourism, trading and logistics, and professional services are the four key industries in Hong Kong, accounting for 60% of the Gross Domestic Product (GDP). The 2009–2010 Chief Executive Policy Address recognized that it is important to constantly enhance the competitiveness of Hong Kong and continue to evolve into a high-value-added, knowledge-based economy to maintain its leading edge over global competitors. The 2020 Chief Executive Policy Address consolidates the city's status as an international financial centre and developing Hong Kong into an international innovation and technology hub as two key economic aims.

6. From 1989 to 2008, Hong Kong's GDP grew at an average annual rate of 4% in real terms. In 2008, the GDP grew by 2.5% in real terms, a rapid deceleration from the strong 6.4% growth in 2007. In 2009, the GDP fell by 2.6% as a result of the global financial crisis, but recovery began in the third quarter of 2009. In 2010, economic recovery became increasingly entrenched, with GDP increasing by 7.1%, year-on-year in real terms. 'The Hong Kong economy has moderated since the second quarter of 2011 amid a slowdown in global demand. After expanding by 5% in 2011, GDP in real terms posted a year-on-year growth of 0.9% in the first half of 2012.' Hong Kong was the world's tenth-largest trading entity in 2012, with the total value of imports and exports exceeding its GDP.[2] The year 2012 witnessed the lowest GDP growth (1.7%) over a decade, from 2005 to 2015, and the Hong Kong economy bounced back in 2013 with a 3.1% growth and a 2.7% growth in 2014.[3] Although the overall 2016 GDP growth rate is slower than that of 2015 in Hong Kong, in the fourth quarter of 2016, the Hong Kong economy experienced the strongest growth with 3.1% advance since the June quarter 2015. The reason behind that increasing growth rate is due primarily to the fact that private consumption and goods exports rose faster, while government spending and investment also expanded further in the last quarter of 2016.[4] Hong Kong's total GDP peaked in 2019 at USD 366.02 billion between 2016 and 2021, up by 0.1% from USD 361.69 billion in 2018. Apparently, the outbreak of the COVID-19 virus, which continues to affect the world from the end of 2019 to 2021, has put the Hong Kong economy under

1. *Hong Kong: The Gritty Underbelly of Consumer Technology*, 22 Jul. 2002 (available at www.apmforum.com/columns/china-recon3.htm).
2. *Economic and Trade Information on Hong Kong*, 28 May 2010 (available at https://www.hkeconomy.gov.hk/en/pdf/er_12q4.pdf). *The World Factbook: Hong Kong*, 3 Jun. 2010 (available at https://www.cia.gov/the-world-factbook/countries/hong-kong/). *Hong Kong: The Facts-Statistics,* Information Services Department, Hong Kong, 2010 (available at www.gov.hk/en/about/abouthk/factsheets/). Chapter 3 of the Hong Kong Year Book 2008 (available at www.yearbook.gov.hk/2008/en/index.html). The latest statistics are available at the Census and Statistics Department HKSAR website at www.censtatd.gov.hk/home/index.jsp.
3. Hong Kong Annual Digest of Statistics 2016, Census and Statistics Department Hong Kong Special Administrative Region, December 2016 (available at http://www.censtatd.gov.hk/hkstat/sub/sp50.jsp?productCode=B1010003).
4. Trading Economics, Hong Kong GDP Annual Growth Rate, 18 Mar. 2017 (available at https://tradingeconomics.com/articles/11162018090003.htm).

load, and Hong Kong's total GDP value has been on a downward trend during these three years. Hong Kong's economy grew 7.9% year-on-year in the first quarter of 2020, ending a six-quarter recession and beating the preliminary figure of 7.8%. Although economic activity remained below pre-pandemic levels, it was the fastest growth in economic output since the quarter that ended in March 2010, amid a sharp recovery in global demand. Merchandise shipments surged 30.2% (versus 5.5% in the fourth quarter), mainly to China, the US and the EU, while services exports declined 8.1% (–28.8%). Meanwhile, purchases of goods from abroad rose 22.7% (versus 6.7% previously), while service imports declined –12.9% (versus –33.9% previously). In addition, government spending grew 6.8% (versus 6.1% previously), private consumption rebounded to 1.6% (versus –6.9% previously) and gross fixed capital formation grew 4.5% (versus 3.6%). The Hong Kong government confirmed its forecast for economic growth of 3.5%–5.5% this year.[5]

7. Hong Kong is the fifteenth largest banking centre in the world in terms of external transactions. It is home to Asia's third-largest stock market and the world's sixth-largest foreign exchange market.[6] The government is committed to promoting Hong Kong as a major international financial centre. Hong Kong has one of the world's most open and transparent investment regimes. It is committed to maintaining a level playing field for foreign and local investors both in law and in business practice. To sustain the favourable business environment, the government's approach remains one of minimum interference and maximum support.

8. The Hong Kong Special Administrative Region (HKSAR) was set up after the transfer of sovereignty from Great Britain to China on 1 July 1997. Today, though the role of the West remains as strong as ever, China plays a greater role than ever in Hong Kong. Politically and economically, Hong Kong is becoming more and more Chinese. However, as a Special Administrative Region of China, Hong Kong enjoys a high degree of autonomy with no change in its lifestyle, except for defence and foreign affairs. The 'one country, two systems' applies. The Joint Declaration of 1984 between Britain and China set out the terms and conditions for the return of Hong Kong to China; the Basic Law,[7] enacted by the National People's Congress of China in 1990, functions as the constitutional basis for Hong Kong's government and legal system since the handover. This provides that the HKSAR will maintain Hong Kong's current legal, social and economic systems and lifestyle.

9. The HKSAR is headed by the Chief Executive, who is advised on major policy decisions by the Executive Council. The HKSAR has a two-tier system of

---

5. Trading Economics, Hong Kong GDP Annual Growth Rate, 20 Oct. 2020 (available at http://www.tradingeconomics.com/hong-kong/gdp-growth-annual).
6. *Hong Kong: The Facts-Financial Services,* Information Services Department, Hong Kong, 2010 (available at www.gov.hk/en/about/abouthk/factsheets/). Chapter 3 of the Hong Kong Year Book *2008* (available at www.yearbook.gov.hk/2008/en/index.html).
7. The Basic Law of the Hong Kong Special Administrative Region of the PRC, adopted at the Third Session of the Seventh National People's Congress on 4 Apr. 1990.

representative government. At the central level is the Legislative Council which legislates, controls public expenditure and monitors the performance of the administration. At the district level, eighteen district councils advise on the implementation of policies in their respective areas. The HKSAR has an independent judiciary. It is responsible for the administration of justice and interpretation of the laws enacted by the legislature.

10. One aspect representing the high autonomy is the continuance of the legal system in Hong Kong. According to the two documents mentioned above, Hong Kong is to remain a common law system for at least fifty years after the handover. In comparison to this, the mainland legal system is classified as a civil law system. The common law, rules of equity, ordinances, subordinate legislation and customary law shall be maintained, except for any that contravene the Basic Law, and subject to any amendment by the legislature of the HKSAR.[8] The HKSAR legislature may also pass new legislation. The national law of the PRC shall not be applied in the HKSAR, except those listed in Annex III to the Basic Law.[9] However, the National People's Congress of the PRC may add or delete from the list of laws in Annex III after consulting the Basic Committee and the HKSAR Government.[10]

11. Hong Kong offers a favourable environment for the development of modern information technology (IT). As a regional trading and services centre, Hong Kong is the place for large volumes of commercial transactions supported by excellent telecommunications and IT infrastructure.

12. In his 1997 Policy Address, the Chief Executive stated his vision to make Hong Kong a leader, not a follower, in the information world of tomorrow. In his 1998 Policy Address, he further emphasized the importance of using IT to help Hong Kong retain its competitive edge and to drive its overall economic expansion. This sentiment is retrieved in the most recent 2020 Policy Address, as Hong Kong strives to be an international innovation and technology hub.

8. Article 8 of the Basic Law.
9. The following national laws shall be applicable: Resolution on the Capital, Calendar, National Anthem and National Flag of the PRC; Resolution on the National Day of the PRC; Order on the National Emblem of the PRC Proclaimed by the Central People's Government (attached: design of the national emblem, notes of explanation and instruction for use); Declaration of the Government of the PRC on the Territorial Sea; Nationality Law of the PRC; Regulations of the PRC Concerning Diplomatic Privileges and Immunities.
10. Article 18 of the Basic Law.

Chapter 2. Telecommunications Infrastructure

13. The role of Hong Kong as the leading business centre in the Asia-Pacific region has much to do with its telecommunications infrastructure, which facilitates domestic and international communications by voice or data. According to the 2020 Network Readiness Index Summit, Hong Kong ranked 24th place in the world, and 6th in the Asia and Pacific region. Of course, the two strengths that influence Hong Kong's overall ranking are Technology and Governance, respectively. Hong Kong has developed an excellent and advanced telecommunications infrastructure with 100% full broadband coverage for commercial buildings and domestic households,[11,12] As of September 2020, the IT usage and penetration survey provided by the Hong Kong Government's Office of the Director of IT shows that mobile subscriber penetration in Hong Kong is as high as 281.2% and household broadband penetration has dropped to 94.9%.

14. The first 3G mobile services were launched in January 2004. Since the launch of 3G mobile services, the take-up rate has grown rapidly. In September 2012, more than 8.86 million mobile phone users were enjoying 3G/4G advanced services such as video calls, video streaming/downloading and interactive real-time gaming. With the launch of the CDMA2000 service in November 2008, visitors can now use roaming services through the CDMA2000 network, in addition to the Global System for Mobile Communications (GSM) 900/1800 and W-CDMA networks. All of these conditions provide an excellent foundation for developing an information-based economy in Hong Kong.[13] Hong Kong's 2G network service officially retires from the stage of history in 2020, and the corresponding 3G network service subscribers are declining precipitously over time, with 3G network service subscribers expected to account for only 8% by 2025. 4G network subscribers are the largest segment from 2018 to 2025, peaking at 82% of total network subscribers in 2020. With the advent of 5G networks, 4G network subscribers are expected to decline to 59% in 2025, down from 33% of 5G subscribers, but still the dominant network service.

15. Hong Kong is the first major city in the world to have a fully digitized telephone network, and it has one of the highest rates of telephone line penetration in the region (a rate of 101.6 residential lines per 100 households in January 2010). As of January 2021, the Hong Kong Census reported that the population of Hong Kong is 7.52 million, with a whopping 6.92 million Internet users, accounting for 92% of the total population of Hong Kong. Compared to last year, the peak of the COVID-19 outbreak, the number of Internet users in Hong Kong increased by 128,000, or

11. *From the Commissioner,* Hong Kong Economic and Trade Office in Washington DC Newsletter, Spring 2008 (available at https://www.cedb.gov.hk/en/sectors/telecommunications.html).
12. *Hong Kong: The Facts-Telecommunications,* Information Services Department, Hong Kong, 2013 (available at http://www.gov.hk/en/about/abouthk/factsheets/docs/telecommunications.pdf).
13. *Ibid.*

about 1.9%.[14] According to the reports issued by the International Telecommunications Union (ITU), Hong Kong ranked second in Asia in 2007 in terms of broadband penetration.[15] Hong Kong has one of the world's most advanced fixed broadband network infrastructures and a fixed broadband penetration rate of 94.9% of households.[16] In the period from 2013 to 2015, almost all sectors in telecommunications services experienced a steady increase, with each total growth of 4.9%, 5.5% and a staggering 23% in 2013, 2014, and 2015 respectively,[17] *see* Table 1.

Table 1 Business Receipts (HKD Million)[18]

	2013	*2014*	*2015*
Public local telephone/facsimile/telegraph/ telegram services	4,973.1	5,203.0	5,546.4
Mobile phone services	27,905.7	29,859.9	42,111.2
Public long-distance telephone services	6,710.3	7,112.0	8,918.3
Other telecommunications services	26,838.9	27,898.8	29,581.1
Total	**66,428.1**	**70,073.7**	**86,157.0**

16. Hong Kong is the largest teleport in Asia. Satellite-based telecommunications and television broadcasting services are provided via 185 satellite earth station antennas providing dedicated relay services.[19] As of December 2020, there are 11 submarine cable systems in Hong Kong.[20]

17. Hong Kong's telecommunications industry is totally privately owned and faces no restrictions on foreign investment. All telecommunication services are open

14. *Ibid.*
15. Chapter 17 of the Hong Kong Year Book 2008 (available at http://www.yearbook.gov.hk/2008/en/pdf/E17.pdf).
16. The Institute for Management Development's World Competitive Yearbook 2020 (available at https://yearbook.gov.hk/2020/en/pdf/E17.pdf).
17. *Key Statistics on Business Performance and Operating Characteristics of the Information and Communications,* Financing and Insurance, Professional and Business Services Sectors 54 (available at http://www.statistics.gov.hk/pub/B10800132015AN15B0100.pdf).
18. Sources: *Key Statistics on Business Performance and Operating Characteristics of the Information and Communications,* Financing and Insurance, Professional and Business Services Sectors 54 (available at http://www.statistics.gov.hk/pub/B10800132015AN15B0100.pdf).
19. *Hong Kong: The Facts-Telecommunications,* Information Services Department, Hong Kong, 2013 (available at http://www.gov.hk/en/about/abouthk/factsheets/docs/telecommunications.pdf).
20. As a major telecommunications and internet hub in the region, Hong Kong has eight submarine cable landing stations and is connected to eleven regional and transcontinental submarine cable systems. It is also connected to the Mainland via twenty overland cables. As of December 2020, the total equipped capacity of external telecommunications facilities was over 122,226 Gbps (available at https://www.ofca.gov.hk/filemanager/ofca/en/content_113/telecommunications.pdf).

for competition, and thus Hong Kong is leading the way towards full liberalization in the Asia-Pacific region[21] (*see* Table 2).

Table 2 Key Telecommunications Statistics[22]

Telecommunications Services	*Quantity*
Mobile network operators (December 2020)	5
Local fixed network operators (December 2020)[a]	27
External fixed telecommunications services providers (December 2020)[b]	214
– Facility-based external fixed network operators (December 2020)[c]	42
– Services-based External Telecommunications Services (ETS) providers (December 2020)[d]	172
Residential fixed-line penetration rate (August 2020)[e]	82.76%
Mobile subscriber penetration rate (September 2020)	281.2%
Mobile subscribers (September 2020)	222,393,559
Internet Services	*Quantity*
Internet service providers (ISP) (December 2020)[f]	263
Registered customer accounts with broadband access (estimated) (September 2020)	2,855,266
Household broadband penetration rate (September 2020)	95%
Public Wi-Fi access points (October 2020)	69,299

* In the above table, some operators are authorized to provide more than one type of service, and therefore the above total number of service providers may be larger than the total number of licensees.

a. Include all licensees authorized to provide facility-based local fixed telecommunications services under fixed telecommunications network services (FTNS) licence, fixed carrier licence (FCL) or unified carrier licence (UCL) using wireline or wireless technology.

b. Include all licensees authorized to provide facility-based ETS under FTNS Licence, FCL, UCL and service-based ETS under services-based operator (SBO) licence.

c. Include all licensees authorized to provide cable-based and non-cable-based ETS under FTNS Licence, FCL and UCL.

d. Include all licensees authorized to provide service-based external fixed telecommunications services under SBO licence.

21. *Hong Kong Economy: Telecommunications*, 3 May 2012 (available at http://hong-kong-economy-research.hktdc.com/business-news/article/Hong-Kong-Industry-Profiles/Telecommunications-Industry-in-Hong-Kong/hkip/en/1/1X000000/1X003VIX.htm).
22. Office of the Telecommunications Authority, Hong Kong (available at www.ofca.gov.hk/en/media_focus/data_statistics/key_stat/).

e. The number of residential fixed-line refers to the total number of residential exchange lines and non-exchange lines, while the residential fixed-line penetration is calculated by dividing the number of residential fixed lines by the number of households in Hong Kong.

f. Include all licensees authorized to provide Internet access services under FCL, UCL, and SBO licence.

Chapter 3. The Information and Communications Technology Market

18. Hong Kong's IT market is one of the most developed in the region. It has some of Asia's largest and most sophisticated computer installations. In 2020, there were over 2 million households with personal computers (PCs) in Hong Kong, accounting for over 75% of all households. The number of households with computers in 2020 is down from 2017.[23] As in mainland China, for many people from Hong Kong, cell phones are the primary device for Internet access, reducing the need for a computer at home.

19. With the progressive liberalization in the last few years, the Information Communication and Technology (ICT) market is now characterized by open and effective competition, voluntary and industry-led standards and wide consumer choices. The combination of computers and telecommunications technology is creating new applications and services in Hong Kong. A study conducted by the Office of the Telecommunications Authority (OFTA) in October 2008 found that the take-up rates of fixed voice services, mobile services, broadband services and data services in Hong Kong are in the top tier among all the Organisation for Economic Co-operation and Development (OECD) economies. Hong Kong also had the most affordable mobile and fixed telecom services.[24]

20. In 2020, households with access to the Internet at home constituted 93.9% of all households in Hong Kong. The robust growth in the Internet market is largely attributable to the popularity of broadband access services and the widespread use of mobile broadband services. In 2020, the number of fixed broadband Internet access lines reached 38.4 per 100 population in Hong Kong. The corresponding figure for mobile broadband subscriptions was much higher, being 307.41 per 100 population.[25]

21. ISPs are very important in providing access to the basic infrastructure and services for content hosting. In Hong Kong, the ISP market is highly competitive. There are now around 193 ISPs in operation in Hong Kong.[26] The ISP market is dominated by a few major players. In November 1996, the Hong Kong Internet Service Providers Association (HKISPA) was formed to promote the development of the Internet. The member companies of the HKISPA account for over 75% of Hong Kong's Internet user market.

---

23. Thematic Household Survey Report No. 73, Census and Statistics Department, April 2021 (available at https://www.ogcio.gov.hk/en/about_us/facts/doc/householdreport2021_73.pdf).
24. Chapter 17 of the Hong Kong Year Book 2008 (available at www.yearbook.gov.hk/2008/en/index.html).
25. Hong Kong as an Information Society (2021 Edition) (https://www.censtatd.gov.hk/en/data/stat_report/product/B1110006/att/B11100062021AN21B0100.pdf).
26. Office of the Telecommunications Authority, Hong Kong (available at www.ofca.gov.hk/en/media_focus/data_statistics/key_stat/).

22. As of December 2020, Hong Kong has eleven submarine cable systems for external connections. Accordingly, consumers enjoy the choice of a wide and sophisticated range of services at competitive prices. Broadband access of speeds up to 1,000 Mbps to the Internet is available, ahead of some areas in the US and Europe. Hong Kong is also a world leader in the deployment of Fibre-To-The-Home (FTTH) and Fibre-To-The-Building (FTTB) technologies. Thus, contact with consumers and suppliers in Asia is cheap and convenient in Hong Kong.

23. Broadband access is very popular in Hong Kong. All local fixed carriers are allowed, under their licences, to provide broadband services using asymmetric digital subscriber line asynchronous digital subscriber loop, FTTH, FTTB, hybrid fibre coaxial cable, local multipoint distribution system (LMDS) and other technologies. Other than the traditional wireline-based broadband service, there has been an increasingly widespread of wireless local area networks (WLAN) since 2008. To promote smart city development, the Government has been actively promoting Wi-Fi.HK service with a view to providing free public Wi-Fi services with better user experience for the public and tourists. HK branded hotspots have already exceeded 36,000 in airports, tourist attractions, restaurants, shopping malls and stores, banks, youth service centres and self-study rooms, and have been extended to over 3,000 buses and cabs, as well as non-fixed Wi-Fi hotspots such as the Airport Express. Wi-Fi.HK has also been fully installed in the sitting-out areas of 185 public housing estates and all public hospitals.[27]

24. Analysed by employment size of establishments, the proportion of establishments using the Internet was higher for large and medium establishments (100% and 98%, respectively) than for small establishments (89%). This reflected that the Internet had become an important means of communication, particularly in large and medium establishments. The Internet is widely used in the business sector of Hong Kong. Around 90% of all establishments use the Internet. Analysed by industry grouping, the proportion of establishments using the Internet was the highest in the information and communications sector (100%) and lowest in the transportation, storage and courier services sectors (76%).[28] There are about 300,000 small and medium-sized enterprises (SMEs) in Hong Kong.[29] Application Services Providers (ASPs) deliver and manage applications and computer services from remote data centres to multiple users via the Internet or a private network. It is expected that SMEs would benefit most from ASP services so as to concentrate their

27. Census & Statistics Dept., *Report on 2009 Annual Survey on Information Technology Usage and Penetration in the Business Sector*, 21 Dec. 2009 (available at http://www.statistics.gov.hk/pub/B11100052009AN09B0200.pdf).
28. *Report on the Survey on Information Technology Usage and Penetration in the Business Sector for 2019* (available at https://www.censtatd.gov.hk/en/data/stat_report/product/B1110005/att/B11100052019BE19B100.pdf).
29. Trade & Indus. Dept., http://www.tid.gov.hk/english/smes_industry/smes/smes_content.html.

resources on their core businesses. Besides technical support, the ASPs in Hong Kong also provide integrated e-commerce solutions such as supply chain management to clients.[30]

25. The number of Internet users has grown by leaps and bounds, and various tasks are being performed via the Internet. As of December 2016, Hong Kong had over 5.4 million Internet users. Internet traffic over broadband networks reached 851,174 terabits by April 2021[31] (*see* Tables 3 and 4).

Table 3 Business Receipts of Internet Connection Services (HKD Million)[32]

	2013	*2014*	*2015*
Basic connection services[a]	9,162.7	8,075.6	9,951.8
Advertising and website hosting services	1,771.2	2,169.3	1,620.5
Other services	4,997.2	4,828.5	3,467.8
Total	**15,931.1**	**15,073.4**	**15,040.2**

a. Including dial-up/leased line/broadband accounts, excluding membership/registration/account set-up services.

Table 4 Percentage of Establishments with Internet Connections[33]

By Industry		*By Employment Size*	
Manufacturing, electricity & gas	89.1%	Large	100%
Construction	92.3%	Medium	98%
Import/export, wholesale and retail trades, & accommodation and food services	88.2%	Small	89%
Transport, storage & courier services	75.9%		
Information and communications	100.0%		

30. *Hong Kong Economy: Internet*, 8 Sep. 2009 (available at www.hktdc.com/info/vp/a/hke/ en/1/5/1/ 1X0060U6/Internet.htm#).
31. Office of the Telecommunications Authority, Statistics of Internet Traffic Volume (available at http: //www.ofca.gov.hk/filemanager/ofca/en/content_293/cus_isp_en.pdf), http://www.internetlivestats.c om/internet-users/china-hong-kong-sar/, and http://www.ofca.gov.hk/en/media_focus/data_statistics/ internet/customer_access_via_broadband_networks/index.html.
32. Source: *Key Statistics on Business Performance and Operating Characteristics of the Information and Communications, Financing and Insurance, Professional and Business Services Sectors in 2011*, at 55 (available at http://www.statistics.gov.hk/pub/B10800132011AN11B0100.pdf).
33. Source: *Report on the Survey on Information Technology Usage and Penetration in the Business Sector for 2019,* Census and Statistics Department, February 2020 (available at https:// www.censtatd.gov.hk/en/data/stat_report/product/B1110005/att/B11100052019BE19B100.pdf).

By Industry		*By Employment Size*	
Financing, insurance, real estate, professional & business services	95.9%		
Social and personal services	92.7%	Overall	90%

Chapter 4. e-Commerce: Facts and Figures

§1. Development of Internet-Based e-Commerce

26. Internet-based Electronic Data Interchange (EDI) solutions are now available and affordable in Hong Kong. They offer a cost-effective alternative to traditional EDI without the need for private networks. Internet-based EDI uses Web Browser interfaces for input and display and then converts the message to the EDI format for transport via private value-added networks. As a result, smaller firms and temporary business partners who need to participate in the larger organization's EDI network need only invest in a PC, a modem and a browser. Many network providers offer packages to SMEs and NGOs. This is favourable to the majority of merchants in Hong Kong.

27. Over 90% of Hong Kong's businesses are small businesses, almost all of which are family owned. With highly flexible supply networks that allow them to produce goods better, faster and cheaper, many Hong Kong businesses have been transferring to the new area with more advanced technologies. e-Commerce, business conducted over the Internet, is growing at a phenomenal rate. Hong Kong has witnessed tremendous progress in its development and adoption of e-commerce during the past years.

§2. Types of e-Commerce

28. Two types of e-commerce are generally identified. Business-to-Consumer (B2C or consumer online transaction) is the sale of goods or services to final consumers over the Internet which can include online stores and sites offering financial services (particularly banking and securities), ticketing services and information services. The major barriers to this type of e-commerce in Hong Kong are concerns about security and whether online retailers are trustworthy and can fulfil their promises. According to a survey conducted by MasterCard Worldwide, online purchasing by consumers is very limited in Hong Kong, as a mere 35.8% of persons aged 15 or above have used online purchasing services for personal matters in 2018.[34]

29. Another type of e-commerce is the so-called Business-to-Business (B2B), which involves companies doing business with the assistance of the Internet. The EDI has been used for this widely for quite some time in Hong Kong. A number of B2B websites have been established in Hong Kong, usually involving standard commodity trading such as steel, sourcing activities or supply chain management.

34. *Hong Kong Economy: Internet* (available at https://www.legco.gov.hk/research-publications/english/1920issh34-e-commerce-in-hong-kong-20200708-e.pdf).

e-Commerce usage is also very limited in the business sector. In 2018, business receipts from Internet sales amounted to HKD 491.7 billion.[35]

§3. Development of e-Commerce via Mobile Devices

30. e-Commerce conducted via mobile devices, such as phones and Personal Digital Assistants (PDAs), is an increasingly common practice for the citizens of Hong Kong. Global e-commerce sales have grown over the past four years from just under USD 1 trillion in 2016 to nearly USD 3 trillion in 2020. Based on this increasing trend, total e-commerce sales are expected to reach USD 3.56 trillion by 2021. Such mobile e-commerce shall consist of the following different market sectors:

(a) automated point-of-sale payments (vending machines, parking metres and ticket machines);
(b) attended point-of-sale payments (shop counters, taxis);
(c) mobile-accessed Internet payments (merchant Wireless Application Protocol sites);
(d) mobile-assisted Internet payments (fixed Internet sites using phones instead of credit cards);
(e) peer-to-peer payments between individuals.[36]

After the catastrophic Asian Tsunami in early 2006, a special fund-raising event with live television coverage was organized to help raise funds for the victims. Mobile phone subscribers on any network could send a blank SMS to a special number, and the call was charged at HKD 20, which sum was handed on to the charity to help tsunami victims. This also demonstrated the ease with which payments for goods can be made through mobile phone bills if an online payment system is needed.[37]

§4. Internet Banking and Business

31. Internet banking, online stock trading and Internet shopping are becoming part of the community members' daily lives. Businesses in Hong Kong are comparatively aggressive in the use of the Internet. Financial institutions are the most prominent users of e-commerce, and most banks provide online banking. Online share trading is also widespread allowing investors and brokers to trade securities

---

35. Information Technology and Broadcasting, Research Office, Legislative Council Secretariat, Statistical Highlights (available at https://www.legco.gov.hk/research-publications/english/1920issh34-e-commerce-in-hong-kong-20200708-e.pdf).
36. For further information, *see* D. Legard, *M-Commerce to Be $25B Market by 2006* 22 Mar. 2002 (available at www.computerworld.com.au/article/25480/study_m-commerce_25b_market_by_ 2006 /).
37. R. Milburn, *Hong Kong Leads Asia in Communications Convergence*, in *2007 Official Guide to Communications in Hong Kong*, Commun. Assn. H.K. (available at https://www.cahk.hk/ publications).

electronically through the Internet, mobile phones and other electronic channels.[38] According to figures released by the Census and Statistics Department, business establishments with a web presence is around 30% as of 2019.[39]

32. The Economist Intelligence Unit ranks Hong Kong's e-business readiness as eighth out of the seventy countries surveyed in 2009. Hong Kong has also embraced smart card technology, with the use of e-money smart cards for payment in transport and retail services in everyday life. The Hong Kong Government introduced smart identity cards in 2003 which can support multiple applications, and new smart ID in 2018 which promotes the usage of e-channels and security protection.[40]

§5. E-COMMERCE PROVIDERS

33. Hong Kong was among the first places in Asia to embrace e-commerce. Among the largest e-commerce providers are:

- *Tradelink*, the pioneer of e-commerce, has been promoting paperless trade and fully supporting e-commerce for Hong Kong's businesses since the launch of its first electronic service in 1997. Tradelink built a superb reputation and recognition across a broad range of industries and became one of the most influential e-commerce service providers in Hong Kong. Its wholly-owned subsidiary, Digi-Sign Certification Services Ltd., appeared to be the first certification authority (CA) company in the country, providing a highly secure and trusted environment for its customers to conduct online transactions. Tradelink's Digital Trade and Transportation Network Ltd. provides an open, neutral, reliable and trusted community e-platform for trade, logistics and finance industries, enabling fast and efficient communications, document exchanges and information sharing among all scales of businesses (tradelink-ebiz.com). Tradelink also provides a range of value-added, transaction-management facilities, including message checking, matching and validation, message authentication and security, electronic billing and payments, message archiving and audit-trail services.
- *e-Shopping* has been providing customers with the ability to build their own online e-shop, supplying a choice of over forty Professional e-Shop Designs; it also supports a variety of management services, such as web-based easy control panel management, customer management, order and invoice management, product and category management, newsletter shipping management and discount management. Payment systems supported by e-Shopping are PayPal, WorldPay, Paydollar, HKBea and PayLink (homepage.com.hk).

---

38. *Hong Kong: Telecoms and Technology Report*, in *Industry Report: Telecoms and Technology*, The Economist Intelligence Unit (October 2009).
39. Census and Statistics Department, Report on Annual Survey on Information Technology Usage and Penetration in the Business Sector, 2019 (available at https://www.censtatd.gov.hk/en/data/stat_report/product/B1110005/att/B11100052019BE19B100.pdf).
40. Chapter 17 of the Hong Kong Year Book 2008 (available at www.yearbook.gov.hk/2008/en/index.html). Digital 21 Strategy, *Measurement of ICT Development under the 2008 Digital 21 Strategy* (available at www.info.gov.hk/digital21/eng/statistics/stat.html).

- *EZ Trade*, offered by a private group, the Hong Kong Article Numbering Association, supplies with EDI solutions that conform to international standards and automate the flow of papers between trading partners.
- *Hongkong Post e-Cert*, a recognized CA, supplies with a digital certificate that is stored in the smart identity card held by every Hong Kong resident, individual and organization.[41]
- *Global e-Trading Services* (www.ge-ts.com.hk) can accept filings of import and export declarations, applications for dutiable commodities permits, electronic submission of cargo manifests and services and bill payments for port security charges.[42]

§6. Overview

34. Though the development of e-commerce has been spectacular during the last few years, it is fair to say that e-commerce is still at an early stage in Hong Kong. 9% of Hong Kong companies have sold goods, services or information through electronic means in 2020 (compared to 1.1% in 2000 and 1.5% in 2009). Such transactions accounted for 1.69% of their total business receipts in 2008 (compared to 0.17% in 2000).[43] However, in recent years, the application of electronic means in selling goods, services or information experienced a steady increase. In 2019, 5.7% (amounted to HKD 40,058 billion) of the total business receipts of all selected industry sectors were conducted through electronic means[44] (*see* Table 5).

Table 5 Industry Data[45]

	2018	*2019*	*2020*
Population (million)	7.48	7.5	7.47
Number of Internet users (million)	6.39	6.53	6.60
Internet penetration rate	85.4%	87%	88.3%
e-Commerce business receipts (HKD million)	n/a	40,058	n/a

41. *Internet and E-Commerce Industry in Hong Kong*, 3 Aug. 2009 (available at http://ecommercejournal.com/articles/17185_internet_and_e_commerce_industry_in_hong_kong).
42. *Country Commerce: Hong Kong*, The Economist Intelligence Unit (October 2009).
43. Census & Statistics Dept., Report on 2009 Annual Survey on Information Technology Usage and Penetration in the Business Sector, 21 Dec. 2009.
44. Source: Report on the Survey on Information Technology Usage and Penetration in the Business Sector for 2015, Census and Statistics Department, March 2016 (available at http://www.statistics.gov.hk/pub/B11100052015BE15B0100.pdf).
45. Source: Report on the Survey on Information Technology Usage and Penetration in the Business Sector for 2019, Census and Statistics Department, February 2020 (available at https://www.censtatd.gov.hk/en/data/stat_report/product/B1110005/att/B11100052019BE19B100.pdf) and http://www.https://www.statista.com/statistics/973717/hong-kong-internet-penetration-rate/.

Chapter 5. e-Government Initiatives

§1. Basic Understanding

35. Since the late 1980s, the Hong Kong Government has cooperated with the private sector to ensure the success of e-commerce in Hong Kong. For example, the government took an interest in Tradelink, an e-commerce company that worked to promote submission of trade-related government applications, including export licence requests and textile production documents, in electronic form. e-Government in Hong Kong was first introduced in 2001 under the Digital 21 Strategy with the initial policy objectives of 'publishing information online' and 'supporting electronic transactions'. More recently, in the 2014 Digital 21 Strategy, the Government has committed to enhancing 'multi-platform government services' to enable the public to access information and services anytime, anywhere, on any device and any platform. It has also committed to providing 'integrated two-way e-services' where more personalized and customized e-services are now technically feasible through the application of big data analytics.

36. e-Government is about shifting the focus from technology to the people who use it. It is about helping individuals, businesses and the community turn possibility into reality. e-Government can provide new and easy ways for the community to participate and access a myriad of services and information more efficiently and effectively. Advancements in technology are enabling the government to deliver better services in a more efficient and effective manner.

37. The HKSAR Government, with the purpose of encouraging even wider use of the Internet and e-commerce, is committed to becoming a model user of IT and has indeed launched the Electronic Tendering System in April 2000 to provide a secured electronic means for handling tender and related matters to support government electronic procurement.[46] With the initiatives of e-government, several advantages can be achieved:

(a) services all day, every day – counter/office opening hours are a thing of the past;
(b) 'one-stop-shop' – one simple stop opens the door to a variety of services;
(c) no more queues – go online instead of standing in line;
(d) comprehensive information; more and faster information at one's fingertips; and
(e) more options – many service channels for convenience: be it e-mail, fax, telephone, kiosk, the Internet through computers or mobile devices or person-to-person by visiting the offices. Customers can make their own choices.

---

46. Info. Tech. & Broadcasting Bureau, *APEC E-commerce Readiness Assessment Guide-A Self-assessment on Hong Kong's Readiness for E-commerce*, October 2000 (available at https://www.apec.org/publications/2000/12/apec-ecommerce-readiness-assessment-guide-2000).

§2. Ongoing Efforts

38. The government has launched the Electronic Service Delivery (ESD) Scheme: Government-to-Citizen and Government-to-Business, in order to provide a wide range of public services to the community through the Internet and other electronic means.[47] Such electronic services include the submission of tax returns, renewal of driving and vehicle licences, payment of government bills, and voter registration. Services will be provided twenty-four hours a day, seven days a week, in a public-oriented approach instead of the conventional department-based format.

39. The public can access ESD services through a wide range of delivery channels, including PCs with Internet connection, public information kiosks and any other electronic means. The Internet services were launched on 9 December 2000, while full services (including public information kiosks) were launched on 19 January 2001. The features of this infrastructure are as follows:

(a) it enables the public to obtain services through various channels, including but not limited to PCs, interactive public payphones or television;
(b) the facilities are interoperable, secure and reliable. Using the facilities provided and following the interface standards, one can use diverse access means to obtain services provided by different agencies. This is a more efficient and effective alternative to the conventional form of public service delivery – an alternative as secure and reliable as the conventional, paper-based form;
(c) the interface standards used in the infrastructure are open, market-based standards. This is an important feature to prevent being locked into a particular non-sustainable solution and to ensure that necessary flexibility is built in so as to accommodate more advanced technology in the future;
(d) the user interface of this infrastructure is bilingual. Being a bilingual society, both Chinese and English interfaces are needed for the successful implementation of ESD.[48]

40. Online services offered by ESD Life's website were transferred in January 2008 to www.gov.hk owing to the expiry of the contract between the government and the operator of ESD Life. The website 'www.gov.hk' is now the entry portal for all government information services. Through the GovHK website, residents of Hong Kong can go online to handle most of their government-related business, from paying taxes to booking appointments at the Immigration Department or the local tennis court. An amendment to the Immigration Ordinance approved by the Legislative Council in June 2005 allows even non-permanent residents, as well as permanent Hong Kong residents, to breeze through immigration clearance by swiping their smart identity cards at Automated Passenger Clearance Channels at Hong

47. This effort won the Stockholm Challenge Award, an international IT-award programme organized annually by the City of Stockholm, Sweden. It won the first prize under the category 'Public Services and Democracy' due to its innovative business model to integrate public and commercial services into one single portal.
48. Available at https://www.ogcio.gov.hk/en/news/publications/doc/1998_digital21.pdf.

Kong ports.[49] This is a clear gesture that the government fully supports the development of e-commerce in Hong Kong. The Hong Kong Government was well-known for its political economy that followed the ethos of laissez-faire. This policy was in fact what government officials called 'a positive but non-interventionist policy'.[50]

41. The HKSAR Government fully recognizes the strategic importance of promoting the development of e-commerce for Hong Kong's long-term benefit. It is committed to providing a favourable environment supported by a sound legal framework to foster the development of e-commerce in Hong Kong. To this end, the government has adopted various measures to promote the development of e-commerce in Hong Kong. The Information Technology and Broadcasting Bureau (ITBB) was set up in April 1998 to lead and coordinate the work of all those in government involved in IT and related areas of broadcasting and telecommunications. To assist ITBB in this task, the Information Infrastructure Advisory Committee (IIAC) was set up in August 1998.[51] The ITBB was renamed the Communications and Technology Branch (CTB) in July 2003,[52] and the IIAC was replaced by the Digital 21 Strategy Advisory Committee in October 2004 as the highest level of government advisory body on IT matters.[53]

42. The Information Technology Services Department (ITSD) has, over the years, developed an integrated government-wide IT infrastructure within uniform design principles, standard models, common facilities and proper measures to safeguard information integrity and security in the government system. It has established in particular a physical backbone network infrastructure to facilitate network connections among bureaux and departments, and a central electronic messaging hub facilitating the sending and receiving of electronic messages among bureaux and departments efficiently. The ITSD has also established a central Internet gateway (CIG) system to enable bureaux and departments to disseminate information, communicate and transact business with the public over the Internet efficiently and under a secure environment. In July 2004, the ITSD and the CTB were merged to form the Office of the Government Chief Information Officer, responsible for formulating policies, and strategies and implementing measures to drive IT development in Hong Kong.[54]

43. The government IT infrastructure has been built up by connecting all bureaux and departments together via the core Government Backbone Network. In addition to this, common applications and services are provided to bureaux and

---

49. *Country Commerce: Hong Kong*, The Economist Intelligence Unit (October 2009).
50. D. Jan, *Building Electronic Commerce Infrastructure: The Hong Kong Retail Sector (A)*, Centre for Asian Business Cases, 5 (U.H.K. 1999).
51. *Digital 21: Hong Kong Special Administrative Region Information Technology Strategy*, November 1998 (available at www.info.gov.hk/digital21/).
52. Press Release, ITBB to be re-titled to CTB, 26 Jun. 2003 (available at http://www.info.gov.hk/gia/general/200306/26/0626194.htm).
53. *Digital 21 Strategy*, HKSAR (available at www.info.gov.hk/digital21/).
54. Available at www.ogcio.gov.hk/.

departments to facilitate the efficient delivery of services to the public. A Government Office Automation programme was completed by the end of 2000 improving the electronic communications within the government. Meanwhile, the Central Cyber Government Office was also set up in August 2000, which is a Government Intranet Service providing a wealth of information and electronic services. The CIG System enables government bureaux and departments to gain access to the Internet, disseminate information, and communicate and transact business with the public over the Internet through a secure and centrally managed gateway.[55]

44. The HKSAR Government is also active in the international arena. It actively participates in international deliberations with entities such as the World Trade Organization (WTO), the Asia-Pacific Economic Cooperation and the OECD in order to keep in close touch with world development and to put across its views on e-commerce. The HKSAR Government has also established bilateral cooperation frameworks with other countries. The aim is to create synergy and establish mutually beneficial relationships among relevant government agencies and industry organizations to enhance ICT development in the respective economies, thereby enhancing our competitiveness and international status in the global knowledge-based economy.[56]

§3. 'Digital 21' and Other Policy Initiatives

45. The then ITBB in conjunction with the then IIAC has formed a package of initiatives called 'Digital 21-Information Technology Strategy' to position Hong Kong as the leader in the digital world of tomorrow. The then Secretary of the ITBB stated, 'we have set out our vision, initiatives and targets of how government, business, industry and the academia can work together to make Hong Kong a leading digital city in a globally connected world'.[57] The proposals include strategies for using a series of top-down initiatives to spur automation while encouraging market forces to drive bottom-up development.[58]

46. Five key themes are identified as follows:

(a) enhance the world-class e-business environment in Hong Kong;
(b) ensure that the Hong Kong Government leads by example;
(c) develop Hong Kong's workforce for the information economy;
(d) strengthen the Hong Kong community for digital exploitation;
(e) leverage Hong Kong's strength in the exploitation of enabling technologies.

55. For a list of government IT infrastructure available, please visit http://www.ogcio.gov.hk/en/infrastructure/index.htm.
56. Available at www.ogcio.gov.hk/.
57. K.C. Kwong, *1998 Digital 21 Strategy* (available at www.info.gov.hk/digital21/).
58. W. Foster, S. Goodman & Z. Tan, *The Internet and E-commerce in Greater South China* (Taiwan, Hong Kong, Fujian, and Guangdong) (available at www.isoc.org).

47. The latest 2008 Digital 21 Strategy was introduced in December 2007 with the motto: 'advancing our achievements and seizing new opportunities: building on Hong Kong's position as a world digital city'. The strategy follows a 'Statements of Desired Outcomes' drawn up to make Hong Kong a vibrant digital economy, a centre for advanced technology and innovation as well as a hub for technological cooperation. Maintaining Hong Kong's position as a leader in the use of e-government and as a knowledge-based society is another of its aims. The Hong Kong Government also set up a Task Force on Digital Inclusion (the Task Force) in July 2008. The Task Force chaired by the Government Chief Information Officer will advise the government on the formulation of relevant strategies and initiatives for addressing digital inclusion issues.

48. Besides its 'Digital 21' policy initiative, Hong Kong is leading other governments to the information age through its citywide broadband implementation[59] and the Cyberport.[60] A world-class Cyberport, a hi-tech multimedia hub costing HKD 131 billion, is being developed with private participation. It will be Hong Kong's IT flagship to provide a focal point for these like-minded companies and professionals to develop innovative IT applications, thus building itself up as an international IT centre.

49. The Cyberport will house about thirty large to medium-sized companies and one hundred smaller companies specializing in the development of services and multimedia content to support various industries. Companies at the Cyberport will benefit from a campus-like environment as well as a range of common facilities and services. These include multimedia equipment, data and business centres, exhibition and demonstration areas, and many useful services such as interfaces with universities and liaison networks with venture capitalists.[61] In June 2004, Cyberport won the Intelligent Building of the Year Award 2004 in New York City. This is given to commercial buildings that have used broadband and information systems technology to add demonstrable value in the form of advanced services and value to their tenants.[62]

50. The Cyberport promises a strategic cluster of quality IT companies and professionals. It will be a place to nurture creativity, foster innovation and groom talent.

---

59. OFTA faces challenges in opening up the broadband market to competition without strangling it through a licensing regime.
60. The Cyberport is a private–public venture for helping Hong Kong leverage its capabilities as a transportation and financial centre into becoming a centre for the development of cyberspace. The goal is to provide the office and residential space for high tech ventures and their employees, creating a synergistic environment.
61. *Hong Kong Industry Profiles: Information Technology Services*, 30 Jan. 2012 (available at http://hong-kong-economy-research.hktdc.com/business-news/article/Hong-Kong-Industry-Profiles/Informmation-Technology-Services-Industry-In-Hong-Kong/hkip/en/1/1X000000/1X006NLI.htm).
62. www.cyberport.hk/.

51. In addition to the Cyberport, Hong Kong has another flagship project, namely, the Hong Kong Science Park. That facility provides quality infrastructure and support facilities for innovation and technology development in the focused clusters encompassing electronics, biotechnology, precision engineering and IT/telecommunications industries, and the upgrading of manufacturing and service industry capabilities. It also provides a full-service incubation programme for technology start-ups as well as fosters partnership and collaboration between industry and universities/applied research institutes through consulting, training and research programmes.[63]

§4. A Solid and Flexible Internal Government Infrastructure and Support

52. Internal infrastructure is vital to the implementation of e-government initiatives. In June 2020, 88% of government staff had a computer to facilitate daily tasks;[64] programmes are being introduced to further enhance computer access to all government employees. Moreover, PDAs are being introduced for officers working outdoors to facilitate off-site operations. Standards and guidelines are constantly refined to ensure that government systems operate smoothly with each other. In 2015, the number of e-government transactions reached over 720 million.[65] By the third quarter of 2016, over 98% of intra-Hong Kong Internet traffic stayed within Hong Kong; Hong Kong's average peak Internet connection speed (at 116.2 Mbps) and average Internet connection speed (at 20.1 Mbps) are among the fastest in the world respectively.[66]

53. Financial support has also increased rapidly to meet the demand. Spending on IT within the government has increased from just over HKD 2,160 million in 1999–2000 to HKD 3,438 million in 2009–2010.[67] The recently updated figure indicates that the government IT expenditures have reached HKD 8,591 million in 2019–2020 and estimates expenditures in 2020–2021 at HKD 10,082 million.[68] Within ongoing projects and new initiatives, it is expected that more financial support will continue to be expended and increased. All those arrangements have important effects on the furtherance of seamless e-government and enable the government to communicate more effectively with the community.

---

63. Speech by D. Pescod, *JP Permanent Secretary for Commerce and Economic Development (Communications and Technology)* at the Cultural Night@Cyberport of ASOCIO ICT Summit 2008, 10 Dec. 2008 (available at http://cvcf.cyberport.hk/cvcf/content/opening-remarks-mr-duncan-pescod-jp-permanent-secretary-commerce-and-economic-development-hk).
64. Office of the Government Chief Information Officer, HKSAR, *Facts and Figures* (available at http://www.ogcio.gov.hk/en/facts/doc/Fact_Sheet-OGCIO-EN.pdf).
65. Available at https://www.export.gov/apex/article2?id=Hong-Kong-Macau-e-commerce.
66. Office of the Government Chief Information Officer, HKSAR, *Facts and Figures* (available at http://www.ogcio.gov.hk/en/facts/doc/Fact_Sheet-OGCIO-EN.pdf).
67. Office of the Government Chief Information Officer, HKSAR, *Government IT Expenditure* (available at http://www.ogcio.gov.hk/en/facts/government_it_expenditure.htm).
68. *Ibid.*

Part I. Regulation of the ICT Market

Chapter 1. Regulatory Framework of the Telecommunications Sector

§1. Regulatory Background

54. 'Telecommunications' is defined as 'any transmission, emission or reception of communication by means of guided or unguided electromagnetic energy or both, other than any transmission or emission intended to be received or perceived directly by the human eye'.[69] The telecommunications sector is a dynamic industry due to both technological change and commercial development. The telecommunications services in Hong Kong are provided by the private sector. The telecommunications market is one of the most open and liberalized in the world. No foreign ownership restrictions exist in this area, and it is the policy of the HKSAR Government that there should be a level playing field in this regard.[70]

55. The government adopts pro-competition and pro-consumer telecommunications policies with the objectives:

(a) that the widest range of quality telecommunications services should be available to the community at reasonable costs;
(b) that telecommunications services should be provided in the most economically efficient manner possible;
(c) that Hong Kong should serve as the pre-eminent communications hub for the region.

56. One major government body, the OFTA, established in 1993 as an independent department and the executive arm of the Telecommunications Authority (TA), is responsible for regulating the rapidly developing and increasingly competitive telecommunications industry in Hong Kong.[71] The work of OFTA covers four main areas:

---

69. Section 2 of the Telecommunications Ordinance.
70. R.B. Chong & W. Chow, *Financing Telecommunications Projects in Asia: A Promising Regulatory Perspective,* 52 Fed. Commun. L.J. 9–11 (December 1999).
71. General Trends in Telecommunication Reform 1998: Asia Pacific Volume V, ITU, compiled in General Trends in Telecommunication Reform 1998: World Report, at 81 tbl.5.2 (1998).

(a) regulation of telecommunications services and equipment;
(b) enforcement of fair competition;
(c) radio frequency spectrum management and satellite coordination;
(d) advisory and planning services.

However, OFTA ceased to function on 31 March 2012. Its powers and duties are transferred to the Office of the Communications Authority, the executive arm and secretariat of the Communications Authority.[72]

§2. Legal Framework

57. The OFTA administers the Telecommunication (Cap. 106), Telephone (Cap. 269) and Outer Space Ordinances (Cap. 523) which govern the establishment and operation of all telecommunications services. The OFTA has established several Advisory Committees to advise on related technical matters such as regulatory matters, matters relating to the radio spectrum frequency, administration of telecommunications numbering and technical standards.[73]

58. The Telecommunications Ordinance was first drafted in 1936 to govern the licensing of radio communication services. Comprehensive amendments were made in 1996, 1998, 2000, 2003, 2010, 2012, 2014 and 2020. Major improvements have been made to enhance competition safeguards, improve the interconnection and access arrangements, streamline the licensing framework and provide powers to the TA on certain technical matters.

59. All licensees of telecommunications services, including those whose licences are granted under section 8 of the Television Ordinance, are governed by the Telecommunication Ordinance.[74] These include specifically FTNS Licences, Public Non-Exclusive Telecommunications Service and Public Radio communication Service licences. With the distinction between fixed and mobile networks and services becoming increasingly blurred, in 2008, a UCL was introduced as a single licensing vehicle for fixed, mobile and/or converged services.[75] In October 2009, the TA announced the introduction of a single, streamlined licensing regime for regulation of all service-based public telecommunications services.[76]

72. Available at https://www.coms-auth.hk/en/about_us/secretariat/index.html.
73. Current Advisory Committees are the Regulatory Affairs Advisory Committee, Radio Spectrum Advisory Committee, Radio Spectrum Advisory Committee, Technical Standards Advisory Committee and Telecommunications Users and Consumers Advisory Committee.
74. *See*, e.g., *Uniglobe Telecom (Far East) Ltd. v. HKSAR* [1999] 2 HKC 147, at 147–148.
75. Chapter 17 of the Hong Kong Year Book 2008 (available at www.yearbook.gov.hk/2008/en/index.html);*Telecom Milestones* (available at https://www.gov.hk/en/theme/bf/consultation/pdf/08005_cp.pdf), under the section of 2008, the second bulletin number.
76. Office of Telecommunications Authority (available at http://tel_archives.ofca.gov.hk/en/telecom_fact/milestones/main.html), under the section of 2009, the sixth bulletin number.

60. This ordinance covers many technical aspects in relation to the use of telecommunications apparatus and lines. It also gives the TA power to determine the terms and conditions of interconnection, to issue directions requiring licensees to take action to comply with their licence conditions or in relation to interconnection, etc., and to impose financial penalties on a licensee for failure to comply with any direction.

61. The Telephone Ordinance was originally nothing more than a monopoly franchise agreement between the Hong Kong Telephone Company (HKTC) and the British Colonial Government. It was substantially modified in 1995 ending HKTC's exclusivity over local service and asserting government control over telephone numbering. This is important in removing barriers for the new entrants to compete for customers as number portability allows customers of the HKTC to retain their telephone number when they change the service provider or address.[77]

§3. Licensing Regimes

62. Licensing is a basic controlling mechanism for the HKSAR Government. An exclusive licence can be issued by the Chief Executive of Council, who may:

(a) determine the conditions of the licence including (but not limited to) the period of validity, the payment of fees and royalties, and the frequency of any payments;
(b) grant the licence; and
(c) publish notice of the grant of the licence as he sees fit.[78]

63. Licences other than exclusive licences and carrier licences can also be issued. The authorities may determine the form of licences; the conditions of licences; the period of validity of the licences as well as the types of licences, including class licences to be issued. The authorities also determine fees payable, including for the grant and renewal of licences as well as annual fees.[79]

64. Generally, conditions that may be prescribed for or attached to a licence may relate to the manner of service provision; interconnection, interference with or adherence to technical standards; compliance with directions, guidelines, codes of practice, regulations, the ordinance and international obligations; universal service obligations; accounting practices; the provision of information; tariffs; network coordination; protecting customer information; prohibiting unfair market practice; regulation of a dominant licensee; and the provision of performance bonds.[80]

---

77. Consumer Council, Achieving Competition in the Liberalized Telecommunications Market.
78. Section 7(1) of the Telecommunications Ordinance.
79. Section 7(6) of the Telecommunications Ordinance.
80. Section 7(7) of the Telecommunications Ordinance.

65. Without a proper licence, no person in Hong Kong or on board any ship, aircraft or space object that is registered or licensed in Hong Kong shall:

(a) establish or maintain any means of telecommunications;
(b) offer, in the course of business, a telecommunications service;
(c) possess or use any apparatus for radio communications or any apparatus of any kind that generates and emits radio waves notwithstanding that the apparatus is not intended for radio communications;
(d) deal, in the course of trade or business, in apparatus or material for radio communications, or in any component part of any such apparatus, or in apparatus of any kind that generates and emits radio waves whether or not the apparatus is intended, or capable of being used, for radio communications; or
(e) demonstrate, with a view to sale in the course of trade or business, any apparatus or material for radio communications.[81]

66. The OFTA is empowered to issue licences specified in Schedule 1 of the Telecommunication Regulations. Four types of licence are defined in section 7 of the ordinance: exclusive licences, carrier licences, class licences and other licences not included in the first three types.

§4. Liberalization of the Telecommunications Sector

67. Following the expiry of HKTC Ltd.'s franchise on 30 June 1995, three more operators – Hutchison Global Crossing Ltd., Wharf New T and T Limited and New World Telephone Limited – were licensed to compete with the incumbent operator in the local FTNS market.

68. Hong Kong undertook commitments under the Uruguay Round of the WTO on liberalizing both the value-added and basic telecommunications market. The commitments under the agreement include:

(a) allowing access to the local market;
(b) allowing international simple resale for facsimile and data transmission services;
(c) permitting call back and other alternative international calling services, certain satellite services, virtual private networks and mobile satellite services; and
(d) conforming to the Reference Paper on Regulatory Principles.

69. Hong Kong implemented all of its commitments by 1 January 1998. Nevertheless, the government introduced further competition in the local fixed telecommunications market in 2000, all of which have been well ahead of the commitments made under the WTO.

---

81. Section 8(1) of the Telecommunications Ordinance.

70. Hong Kong Cable Television Limited was licensed to offer telecommunications services over its hybrid fibre coaxial cable network. Five licences were also issued for the provision of fixed telecommunications services using wireless networks (i.e., LMDS technology) in early 2000.[82] Accordingly, new avenues for convergence of voice and data communications services and video content from various providers using different technologies were opened.

71. Moreover, in January 2002, the government invited applications for new local wireless-based FTNS for operation beginning in 2003. As of February 2010, SmarTone Communications Limited was the only licensed local wireless FTNS operator.

72. Another area of liberalization is the external telecommunications facilities market. As of March 2021, there were forty-two licensees permitted to operate either satellite-based external telecommunications facilities or cable-based external telecommunications facilities.[83]

73. To realize the goal of full liberalization, an important agreement was reached between the government and Cable and Wireless Hong Kong Telecommunications Limited (HKT Ltd.) and its group of companies (including Cable and Wireless HKT International Ltd.). The latter voluntarily ended its exclusive licence for certain external telecommunications circuits and services on 31 March 1998. This significant agreement marked the step to full liberalization of service-based external telecommunications markets. As of March 2021, there were 210 ETS operators licensed to operate. Competition has resulted in a substantial reduction in International Direct Dialling call rates and improved quality of services.[84]

The mobile telecommunications market is also a strategic field for liberalization, subject only to spectrum constraint. As of July 2021, there were twenty-seven licensees permitted to provide local fixed carrier services and four mobile network operators.[85] Acknowledging the benefits of the 3G mobile services, the HKSAR Government formulated the policy for licensing of 3G to promote the development of the telecommunications industry, protect consumers' interests, and to maximize benefits to the economy as a whole. In addition to 3G services, all four mobile network operators have deployed 4G services utilising Long Term Evolution technology, enabling mobile service subscribers to enjoy data downlink speeds of up to 450 Mbps.[86]

---

82. The five local wireless FTNS operators were Hong Kong Broadband Network Limited, SmarTone Broadband Services Limited, Winstar Wireless Hong Kong Limited, Eastar Technology Limited and Hua Nan-Teligent Co. Limited.
83. Available at http://www.ofca.gov.hk/filemanager/ofca/en/content_113/telecommunications.pdf.
84. *Ibid.*
85. *Hong Kong: The Facts-Telecommunications*, Information Services Department, Hong Kong, 2016 (available at http://www.ofca.gov.hk/filemanager/ofca/en/content_113/telecommunications.pdf).
86. *Ibid.*

74. Four 3G network licences[87] were issued in 2001. These were allocated by spectrum auctioning, to be preceded by a pre-qualification exercise which involves setting certain minimum criteria on investment, network rollout, financial capability, etc. Furthermore, an open network access requirement is introduced, requiring 3G network operators to make available 30% of network capacity for interconnection to or access by non-affiliated Mobile Virtual Network Operators (MVNOs) and/or content providers on a non-discriminatory basis by commercial negotiations.[88] On 1 April 2020, three MNOs, i.e., Hong Kong Telecom (HKT), China Mobile Hong Kong (CMHK) and 2 Hong Kong (3HK), launched 5G services in Hong Kong.

75. Hong Kong takes an active part in the activities of international and regional telecommunications organizations, including: the ITU; the Asia-Pacific Cooperation Forum; the Asia-Pacific Telecommunity; the Pacific Telecommunications Council; the International Mobile Satellite Organization; the WTO and various conferences, seminars and exhibitions convened by the private sector in the telecommunications industry.

87. Four licences were awarded to Hong Kong CSL Limited, Hutchison 3G HK Limited, SmarTone 3G Limited and SUNDAY 3G (Hong Kong) Limited.

88. Office of the Telecommunications Authority (available at http://www.ofca.gov.hk/en/media_focus/press_releases/index_id_342.html).

Chapter 2. Regulation of Competition in the ICT Market

§1. General Background

76. One of the largest factors driving e-commerce is the potential to realize enormous cost savings, efficiency, competitive advantages and expanded global reach. Many firms are concerned about surviving and regaining competitiveness in this global arena. Hong Kong is a free port and one of the world's best examples of an 'open market economy'. The HKSAR Government is committed to promoting competition to enhance economic efficiency and free trade, thereby also benefiting consumer welfare.

77. The promotion of competition is based on the Statement on Competition Policy, which may be supplemented by a range of sector-specific measures, where necessary, ranging from licensing conditions, contractual provisions, codes of practice, administrative means, public censure and anti-competition provisions in specific legislation.

78. The following three pro-competition principles are listed in the Statement on Competition Policy:

(a) maximizing reliance on, and minimizing interference with, market mechanism;
(b) maintaining a level playing field;
(c) minimizing uncertainty and fostering confidence in system fairness and predictability by consistent application of policies, transparent and accountable operations and adherence to equitable and non-discriminatory standards and practices.[89]

79. The tremendous growth, investment and innovation associated with the Internet have occurred in an almost entirely unregulated and unprotected environment. And there is a broad consensus that this openness is critical to the Internet's continued worldwide development.[90] Market forces determine wages and prices with price controls limited only to certain government-sanctioned monopolies in the service sector. These policies have spurred high rates of real growth, low unemployment, rising wages and an overall steady increase in the standard of living judged in economic terms. The Hong Kong Government levies no import tariffs. It does impose restrictions on the export of high-technology products to certain countries.

---

89. Statement on Competition Policy (available at https://www.compag.gov.hk/en/statement_on_competition_policy.html).
90. *See*, e.g., Federal Communications Commission 'Digital Tornado' and KPMG (1996).

§2. Governmental Arrangements

80. The Competition Policy Advisory Group, chaired by the Financial Secretary, was established in December 1997 to provide a high-level and dedicated forum to review competition-related issues which have substantial policy or systemic implications and examine the extent to which more competition should be introduced in the public and private sectors. It promulgated a Statement on Competition Policy in May 1998 to provide an overarching policy framework to guide sector-specific efforts to promote competition.[91]

81. The government has introduced competition to the ICT market since the mid-1980s, first in cellular telephony (1985), followed by fixed network (1995). The monopoly on the provision of international circuits and the operation of the international gateway for real-time voice services was terminated in March 1998. With the advantages of competition widely recognized around the world, the government is advocating further progress in the ICT market towards furthering competition. This trend moved forward together with the trend of globalization and liberalization. Hong Kong is one of the most liberalized markets in the world so far.

82. The OFTA has established necessary regulations to accompany a competitive environment. It takes an 'objective cost-based approach' towards setting interconnection charges and requires that the incumbent and former monopoly provider interconnect 'at charges which are based on reasonable relevant costs'.[92] The government introduced on 12 May 1999 a new bill to the Legislative Council with the intent to enhance competition and improve interconnection and access arrangements.[93] Telecommunications (Amendment) Bill 2021 seeks to amend relevant provisions of the Telecommunications Ordinance (Cap. 106) to implement measures proposed in the Review of Telecommunications Regulatory Framework to cater for the application and development of 5G and Internet of Things services.

83. A distributed approach has also been adopted regarding universal service obligations by requiring service providers to pay a percentage of revenues to the incumbent carrier for its universal service expenses.[94] Other measures to promote competition also include the avoidance of cross-subsidization by separating the incumbent operator's services.[95] Through all the measures above, Hong Kong aims to present a positive environment for investment.

91. www.compag.gov.hk.
92. Hong Kong Telecommunications (Pacific) Ltd., Application for Authority Pursuant to s. 214 of the Communications Act of 1934, as amended, to Resell International Private Lines for the Provision of Non-telephonic [*sic*] Service between the United States and Hong Kong, Order and Authorization, 13 FCCR 20050, para. 26, 14 Comm. Reg. (P & F) 50 (1998).
93. *Hong Kong Focus: Will Broadband Succeed in Hong Kong?,* Asia Computer Weekly (2 Aug. 1999).
94. General Trends in Telecommunication Reform 1998: Asia Pacific Volume V, ITU, compiled in General Trends in Telecommunication Reform 1998: World Report, 5.6.2., at 93.
95. Hong Kong Telecommunications (Pacific) Ltd., Application for Authority Pursuant to s. 214 of the Communications Act of 1934, as amended, to Resell International Private Lines for the Provision of Non-telephonic [*sic*] Service between the United States and Hong Kong, Order and Authorization, 13 FCCR 20050, para. 31, 14 Comm. Reg. (P & F) 50 (1998).

84. Licensing has been a basic measure in controlling telecommunication services. The concept that all telecommunications services must be licensed is the fundamental principle underlying Hong Kong's legal regime. In practice, the requirement for licensing has been translated into a regulatory charter between the government and a business seeking to introduce a new communication service or infrastructure. Six distinct functions have been bundled into a single process: registration, resource allocation, entry restriction, service classification, conduct regulation, and taxation and revenue generation.[96]

85. This practice was largely in conflict with Hong Kong's WTO commitments. However, the TA later issued Guidelines to Assist the Interpretation and Application of the Competition Provisions of the FTNS Licence in March 1995 to give the FTNS Licensees a better understanding of how the TA will administer these provisions. This guidance brings Hong Kong's practice in line with its WTO commitments.

§3. Regulation on Discounts to Published Tariffs

86. General Condition 20 of the FTNS Licence, a form of which is contained in Schedule 3 of the Telecommunications Regulations, prohibits a dominant licensee in any market for or which includes a telecommunications service from offering any discount to its published tariffs for a particular telecommunications service.

§4. Ongoing Process

87. In January 2000, the government took further steps in liberalizing the telecommunications market by issuing five wireless local FTNS Licences, thirteen external satellite-based FTNS Licences and one more wireline FTNS Licence. As of 2021, there are 27 satellite-based external FTNS and 42 cable-based external FTNS, 12 mobile network operators, and 24 MVNOs. Moreover, there are 165 ETS operators providing a wide range of value-added services such as an e-mail box, store and forward facsimile and EDI.[97]

88. In January 2002, the government announced that it would fully liberalize the FTNS market from January 2003, and there would be no limit to the number of licences to be issued, nor a deadline for application. Furthermore, there will be no requirement for network rollout or investment. The level of investment will be determined by the market. It is expected that further competition will be introduced to provide better quality services at more competitive prices. This announcement was followed by the issuance of the Extension of the Directions Issued to Reach

96. For discussion, *see* further M. Mueller, *Telecom Policy and Digital Convergence: The Hong Kong Economic Policy Studies Series* 70–74 (City U.H.K. Press 1997).
97. Office of the Telecommunications Authority (available at http://app1.coms-auth.hk/apps/telecom_lic/content/lic_search.asp).

Networks Hong Kong Limited and PCCW-HKT Telephone Limited on 15 March 2002 and 1 June 2002, respectively, pursuant to General Condition 44 of their Fixed Telecommunications Services Licences Regarding Declaration of Non-Dominance in the Market for External Bandwidth Services, 14 March 2003.

Chapter 3. Regulation of Cryptography and Other Dual-Use Goods

§1. General Background

89. Security management for transactions is very important to build confidence on the part of consumers. Among the many security functions of such security systems are arrangements that should aim to:

(a) restrict access to the system to those users in the database;
(b) prevent false authentication of parties' identities;
(c) maintain the secrecy of data while it is not in passage over the communication network;
(d) ensure that the data has not been modified either accidentally or fraudulently while in passage over the network; and
(e) prevent unauthorized access to the provider's central computer system in the database.

90. The purpose of encryption is to ensure authentication and integrity of the message. Authentication refers to the assurance that a message originated from the person who purportedly sent it, and integrity refers to assurance that a message has not been altered or otherwise damaged during the transmission. It is regarded as a popular means of protecting communications transmitted through a potentially hostile environment. The basic mechanism is to take a message and convert it, by use of a key, into information that commonly appears random and unintelligible.

91. Cryptography has been specifically suggested to protect the computer system. It is divided into two major categories: symmetrical key encryption and Public Key Infrastructure (PKI). The former refers to the practice that a key used to encrypt is transmitted to the intended recipient, who uses the same key to convert the encrypted message back to its original form. This entails the risk of sending the key to the intended recipient. Based on the basic technology in the symmetrical key encryption, PKI developed a system which provides a safer means. All cryptographic techniques require the use of 'keys' or a set of numbers used in combination with a formula to encode or decode a message into and out of an unreadable form.

92. Under the PKI, two keys exist – one public and one private – which are mathematically related. Using a private key, a person can send a message that can only be decrypted with that person's public key and no other, thereby ensuring the original message. The private key acts as a digital signature. The message can be decrypted by using the sender's public key. In this way, the recipient can know that the document has been signed by the sender using the private key with which the public key is paired and that the document has not been altered between the time it was signed by the sender and the time it was delivered to the recipient.

§2. Regulations in Hong Kong

93. Hong Kong does not impose restrictions on the use of encryption. Crypto products that are to be connected to the public telecoms network, however, must comply with the relevant TA's network connection specifications.[98]

94. Import and export restrictions on encryption devices do exist in Hong Kong; they are set down in the Import and Export (Strategic Commodities) Regulations which closely follow the Wassenaar Arrangement on Export Controls for Conventional Arms and Dual-Use Goods and Technologies.[99] Generally, a licence is required from the Director General of Trade and Industry for importing or exporting cryptography (symmetric over 56-bit key length), except for personal use or for generally available, unchangeable crypto. Contravening the licensing controls is punishable, on conviction on indictment, with an unlimited fine or seven years' imprisonment, and liable to administrative sanctions.[100]

95. Accordingly, the Regulations do not control:

(a) encryption products used for authentication or digital signature unless they contain encryption on data or files;
(b) equipment where the cryptographic capability for the protection of intellectual property rights is not accessible to users;
(c) all general-purpose civilian cellular radio communications handsets that are not capable of end-to-end encryption;
(d) import or export of a PC pre-loaded with encryption software, as long as the PC and the encryption software are accompanying an individual for his or her personal use.[101]

96. Under the Import and Export Ordinance (Cap. 60), the import and export of strategic commodities require licences issued by the Director General of Trade and Industry.[102] Licence applications should be accompanied by technical specifications/ data sheets of the product concerned to enable the Trade and Industry Department to confirm whether or not the goods are strategic commodities and to assess their sensitivity level. For this purpose, the Trade and Industry Department has introduced a pre-classification service.

---

98. For example, Network Connection Specification for connection of Customer Premises Equipment (CPE) to the Public Telecommunications Network in Hong Kong for Broadband Digital Audio-Visual Services, issued by the Telecommunications Authority (TA), HKTA 2025, Issue 2, February 2003.
99. Cap. 60, sub leg. G.
100. B. Koops, *Crypto Law Survey-Hong Kong Special Administrative Region* (available at http://www.cryptolaw.org).
101. *Questions and Answers Concerning the Import and Export (Strategic Commodities) Regulations (Amendment of Schedule 1) Order 2006*, July 2006 (available at www.stc.tid.gov.hk/).
102. Section 3 of the Import and Export Ordinance.

97. The pre-classification service can advise traders on whether a particular product is a strategic commodity or not based on the information and technical specifications/data sheets provided by the traders. The information from this service shall be retained by the Trade and Industry Department for future reference. Thus, the same product with the same technical details shall not be required for subsequent licence applications.[103]

98. The Trade and Industry Department has further issued a licensing of strategic commodities information sheet outlining the licensing scheme. Two lists are provided in Schedule 1: the Munitions List and the Dual-Use Goods List. The Dual-Use Goods List covers goods such as nuclear materials, facilities and equipment, high-speed digital computers, memory devices made from compound semiconductors, single-mode optical fibre, sophisticated communication systems, etc.

99. For importing or exporting strategic commodities, application should be made by completing the Import Licence Application Form (TID 501) or Export Licence Application Form (TID 502) accompanied by brochures/catalogues giving adequate technical details of the commodities. Further documents or reviews might be needed depending on the commodities in question.[104]

---

103. Strategic Trade Control Circular No. 5/04, *Pre-classification Service on Strategic Commodities*, 8 Apr. 2004 (available at www.stc.tid.gov.hk/).

104. Strategic Commodities Control System, Trade and Industry Department, HKSAR, www.stc.tid.gov.hk/eindex.html.

Chapter 4. Legal Status of Standardization

100. Few product safety standards are required for the domestic Hong Kong market. The Innovation and Technology Commission (ITC) was set up within the then Commerce, Industry and Technology Bureau (now Commerce and Economic Development Bureau) on 1 July 2000 with the mission to spearhead Hong Kong's drive to become a world-class, knowledge-based economy. Its Product Standards Information Bureau (PSIB) promotes awareness of the standards requirements of Hong Kong's major markets, in order to help manufacturers and exporters to understand and to comply with these standards.

101. Besides operating a library of 120,000 product standards, the PSIB also offers technical enquiry and sales services for product standards. It offers a free technical enquiry service on overseas product standards, certification requirements, safety requirements and regulations. The service aims, as far as possible, to assist manufacturers and exporters in the interpretation of the technical content of overseas product standards and requirements and, where appropriate, offer suggestions on ways to better enable a product to meet the requirements.

102. The Standards and Calibration Laboratory (SCL) of the ITC is the custodian of Hong Kong's physical measurement standards and is the authoritative point of reference on measurement matters. The laboratory also provides calibration services in various measurement areas, traceable to the International System of Units (SI). The SCL is a signatory of the Global Mutual Recognition Arrangement for National Measurement Institutes operated by the International Bureau of Weights and Measures. A metric system of units – SI – is being adopted in areas including length, area, volume and capacity, force, pressure and energy/power. The Weights and Measures Ordinance (Cap. 68) offers the best guidance.[105] The Commissioner of Customs and Excise shall have power with detailed regulation of the standards of weights and measures.[106]

103. For e-commerce to fulfil its global promise, global rules are important. The International Standards Organization (ISO) is an important body in regulating the issues of standardization. The standards formulated by this body are being adopted via the Hong Kong Quality Assurance Agency, providing a framework for all types of manufacturing industries. At the moment, the HKSAR Government has been working under the aegis of the ISO on the development of the ISO 10646 standard, which is an international coding standard aimed at encompassing the 'Han' characters of all Asian languages into one single common character set. This is very important to the citizens of Hong Kong. While English and Chinese are languages widely used in Hong Kong, Chinese is the mother tongue of the majority of Hong Kong people. The ESD project has stressed the importance of the bilingual factor in the information age.

---

105. Section 6 of the Weights and Measures Ordinance.
106. Sections 3, 7, 8 and 38 of the Weights and Measures Ordinance.

104. In 2000, the new ISO 10646 standard was released which is an updated version of the one in 1993. It eased the existing limitations of Chinese language computing. The latest version of the ISO 10646 was released in 2020. Even with the existence of the new standard, the fact is that the old standard still continues to exist. Thus, there is a demand for easy-to-use conversion tools capable of supporting different standards, which requires close collaboration between the government, the IT and services industry, and academia.[107]

107. *Digital 21: Hong Kong Special Administrative Region Information Technology Strategy*, November 1998 (available at www.info.gov.hk/digital21/).

Chapter 5. Legal Status of Out-of-Court Dispute Settlement in the ICT Sector

§1. Background

105. Disputes are bound to arise in the commercial world. In the faceless world of e-commerce, many online consumers are concerned about resolving disputes arising out of Internet transactions and how their disputes can be efficiently addressed. Indeed, this has proved to be a major obstacle to e-commerce development. Litigation has been a very important means to resolve disputes. However, the disadvantages of litigation justify the view that it is neither a practical nor an appealing option for e-commerce. This has been one impetus for the development of alternative dispute resolution mechanisms.

106. Online redress is an online form of alternative dispute resolution now being widely discussed. The procedures can be performed totally by electronic means.

§2. Domain Name Dispute Resolution

107. Arbitration is one of the most widely used mechanisms so far. The Hong Kong International Arbitration Centre (HKIAC) has been the main body offering such services. It is an independent non-profit organization established in 1985 to assist disputing parties in solving disputes by arbitration and by other means of alternative dispute resolution. It places great emphasis on providing dispute resolution services in a wide variety of areas, including the areas of intellectual property and IT. The HKIAC has set as one of its goals to be one of the leaders among dispute resolution providers in regard to domain names. In 2001, the HKIAC was appointed as the sole domain name dispute resolution provider for the '.hk ccTLD'.

108. The Asian Domain Name Dispute Resolution Centre (ADNDRC) is one of the four providers in the world – and the first and only one located in Asia – of dispute resolution services in regard to generic top-level domain (gTLD), which are the top-level domains approved by the Internet Corporation for Assigned Names and Numbers (ICANN), which appointed the ADNDRC as a domain name dispute provider on 3 December 2001. The ADNDRC (Hong Kong Office) is operated and managed by the HKIAC.

109. The HKIAC deals with disputes according to the Uniform Domain Name Dispute Resolution Policy (UDRP) and the UDRP Rules approved for implementation by the ICANN on 26 August 1999 and 24 October 1999 as well as the ADNDRC Domain Name Dispute Supplemental Rules adopted by the ADNDRC, effective 28 February 2002.[108]

---

108. It is to be noted that the provisions apply to disputes involving.com.net and.org domain names. Domain names involving '.biz' and '.name' have slightly modified Dispute Resolution Policies.

110. The HKIAC provides domain name dispute resolution services in the following ways:

(a) it serves as partner and manager of the Hong Kong Office of the ADNDRC in regard to '.com', '.net' and '.org' domain names and later to '.biz' and '.name' domain names, and further to other new gTLDs as the latter become operational;
(b) it is the sole provider of dispute resolution services in regard to '.hk' domain names, having been appointed for such purposes by the Hong Kong Domain Name Registration Company Limited (HKDNR). Mandatory final and binding arbitration is the method chosen by the HKDNR for the purpose of resolving disputes in regard to '.hk' domain names;
(c) it has been appointed by the China Internet Network Information Centre to resolve '.cn' domain name disputes;
(d) it has been appointed by the '.pw' Registry Corporation as the sole '.pw' Domain Name Dispute Resolution Service Provider;
(e) it was appointed by the '.dotPH' – the official Domain Name Registry for the Philippines to resolve '.ph' domain name disputes;
(f) it was appointed by Dot Asia Organization on 21 December 2007 as the global official dispute resolution provider to handle disputes and challenges arising out of the launch of the Asia domain.

111. Administrative proceeding is the method specified by the ICANN for the purpose of resolving domain name disputes. This process will essentially be based only on the documents provided by the parties with a face-to-face hearing occurring only in exceptional cases.

112. In order to facilitate the efficient and speedy disposition of domain name disputes, the HKIAC, being technology powered and supported by the Tradelink Electronic Commerce Ltd., has developed a proprietary online domain name dispute resolution system which permits parties to conduct dispute resolution processes by means of a sophisticated, fully online web-based system. The disputing parties can file complaints and exchange views through e-mails, and the case can be handled totally online. Other offline facilities, such as post and fax are also available and allowed in this mechanism.

113. The necessary forms needed to file a complaint and to file a response can be downloaded by clicking on 'Download Form'. Parties can learn more about the whole process by making use of the System User Guide, which is available in the 'Download Forms' area. Furthermore, a 'flow chart of proceedings' is also available to show the various stages of the proceeding, as well as a series of 'Frequently Asked Questions (FAQs)' and answers thereto, which can help educate the potential user of the mechanism.[109]

---

109. Available at https://adndrc.org/mten/home.html.

§3. HKDNR Domain Name Dispute Resolution Policy

114. The HKDNR has adopted a policy to deal with domain name disputes. This policy is almost the same as ICANN's policy and is incorporated by reference into the Domain Name Registration Agreement setting forth the terms and conditions for registration.

115. It is provided that any person or entity may initiate an arbitration proceeding against a registrant to assert the rights to the registered domain name. To initiate the proceeding, the complainant shall be required to provide evidence that: the domain name is identical or confusingly similar to a trademark or service mark in Hong Kong in which the complainant has rights; that the registrant has no rights or legitimate interests with respect to the domain name; and that the domain name should be considered as having been registered and being used in bad faith.[110]

116. Several situations have been listed to show evidence of 'bad faith':

(a) circumstances indicating that the registrant has registered or acquired the domain name primarily for the purpose of selling, renting or otherwise transmitting the domain name registration to the complainant who is the owner of the trademark or service mark or to a competitor of that complainant, for valuable consideration in excess of the registrant's documented out-of-pocket costs directly related to the domain name; or
(b) the registrant has registered the domain name in order to prevent the owner of the trademark or service mark from reflecting the mark in a corresponding domain name, provided that it has engaged in a pattern of such conduct; or
(c) the registrant has registered the domain name primarily for the purpose of disrupting the business of a competitor; or
(d) by using the domain name, the registrant has intentionally attempted to attract, for commercial gain, Internet users to its website or other online location, by creating a likelihood of confusion with the complainant's mark as to the source, sponsorship, affiliation or endorsement of the registrant's website or location or of a product or service on the registrant's website or location.[111]

117. As a defence, the registrant can offer some evidence to show his rights or legitimate interests in the domain name:

(a) before any notice of the dispute, the registrant had used, or is prepared to use, the domain name or a name corresponding to the domain name in connection with a bona fide offering of goods or services in Hong Kong;
(b) the registrant has been commonly known by the domain name, even if no trademark or service mark rights have been acquired in Hong Kong;

110. Article 3 of the HKDNR Domain Name Dispute Resolution Policy (Rules of Procedure), effective 22 Feb. 2011 (available at https://www.hkdnr.hk/en/dispute/rule-of-procedure/).
111. Article 4(b) of the HKDNR Domain Name Dispute Resolution Policy, effective 22 Feb. 2011 (available at https://www.hkdnr.hk/en/dispute/domain-name-dispute-resolution-policies/).

(c) the registrant has trademark or service mark rights that the mark is identical to the domain name the registrant is holding; or
(d) a legitimate non-commercial or fair use has been made of the domain name, without intent for commercial gain to misleadingly divert consumers or to tarnish the trademark or service mark at issue;
(e) if the domain name is registered in one of the individual domain name categories, the domain name registered must be the registrant's own 'individual name'.[112]

118. According to the policy, the HKDNR is exempted from any liability arising from disputes from its services. The HKDNR takes a passive position in the proceedings: remaining silent and taking no actions on the status of the disputed domain name. Only when an order is sent from one dispute resolution provider or the Hong Kong Court will the HKDNR take action. The remedies available to the winner are limited to the cancellation or transfer of the registered domain name.

§4. Rules of Procedure

119. The complaint shall be submitted in electronic form in accordance with the Domain Name Dispute Resolution Policy (DNDRP) and these rules of procedure to any provider that such person or entity may select.[113] The provider should employ reasonably available means calculated to achieve actual notice to the registrant/respondent.[114] The provider shall review the complaint for administrative compliance with DNDRP, the rules of procedure and the provider's supplemental rules. The date of commencement of the arbitration proceeding shall be the date when the provider forwards the complaint to the respondent.[115] The respondent shall have fifteen business days to prepare a response to the provider.[116]

120. A list of panellists and their qualifications shall be available to both parties. If both parties have not elected a three-member Arbitration Panel, the provider shall appoint, within five business days following receipt of the response, a single arbitrator from the list.[117] In the case of a three-member Arbitration Panel, the provider shall appoint one panellist from the list of candidates provided by each party; the third panellist shall be appointed by the provider from a list of five candidates submitted to the parties.[118] Impartiality and independence shall be maintained by the panellists; no unilateral communications shall be made between any party and the

112. *Ibid.*, Art. 4(d).
113. Article 3(a) of the HKDNR Domain Name Dispute Resolution Policy (Rules of Procedure). Effective 22 Feb. 2011 (available at https://www.hkdnr.hk/content.jsp?id=158#!/159).
114. *Ibid.*, Art. 2(a).
115. *Ibid.*, Art. 4(a), (c).
116. *Ibid.*, Art. 5(a).
117. *Ibid.*, Art. 6(b).
118. *Ibid.*, Art. 6(e).

panel.[119] The language used in the registration agreement shall be adopted for the proceedings.[120] In-person hearings are possible, but only at the discretion of the panel in 'exceptional' cases.[121]

121. Generally, decisions shall be made based on the statements and documents submitted. It is important to note that the decision shall be in writing, provide the reasons on which it is based, indicate the date on which it was rendered, and identify the name(s) of the panellist(s).[122]

122. The complainant shall be the primary party to pay an initial fixed fee to the provider. Once the respondent chooses a three-member panel, he or she shall pay one-half of the fixed fee.[123] Except in the case of deliberate wrongdoing, the provider and the panellists are exempted from liabilities for acts or omissions in connection with any arbitration proceeding.[124]

123. The last thing to note is that this arbitration proceeding does not preclude recourse to the courts. A person has a choice between making a complaint to this arbitration proceeding or bringing a suit in a court to challenge a domain name. This rule is also in accordance with the conception of mutual jurisdiction or primacy of litigation advocated in the ICANN DNDRP.[125]

§5. Electronic Transaction Arbitration Rules

124. The Hong Kong Society of Accountants (HKSA) launched the WebTrust Programme in Hong Kong in 2001 providing a worldwide professional assurance standard for e-commerce practice. To ease online consumers' worries and to facilitate dispute resolution matters for both consumers and online business, the WebTrust Programme requires an online merchant to commit to the use of third-party dispute resolution that conforms to the twelve principles of arbitration procedure developed by the National Arbitration Forum (based in the US), and to disclose its procedures for consumer recourse for issues not resolved by it.

125. The HKSA and the HKIAC, sharing similar views on the importance of arbitration as a dispute resolution mechanism for e-commerce, held a joint press conference on 29 January 2002 announcing the launch of the HKIAC Electronic Transaction Arbitration Rules for use and adoption by online merchants in Hong

119. *Ibid.*, Arts 7–8.
120. *Ibid.*, Art. 11(a).
121. *Ibid.*, Art. 13.
122. *Ibid.*, Art. 15.
123. *Ibid.*, Art. 18(a).
124. *Ibid.*, Art. 19.
125. Article 4(k) of the ICANN Uniform Domain Name Dispute Resolution Policy, effective 24 Oct. 1999 (available at www.icann.org/en/udrp).

Kong, and to present the key features of the rules. The rules help parties and arbitrators to take maximum advantage of the flexible procedures available in arbitration for the resolution of disputes quickly and economically. The rules provide a local framework for an arbitration aiming to cover disputes arising from the seven aspects of e-commerce relevant to the WebTrust Programme, namely business practices/transaction integrity, online privacy, security, availability, confidentiality, non-repudiation and CAs.

126. The rules were adopted to take effect from 1 January 2002. As defined by the rules, the arbitrator shall have the power to adopt a simplified or expedited procedure and shall have the widest discretion allowed by law to conduct the proceeding so as to ensure the just, expeditious, economical and final determination of the dispute.[126] This shall be the central point guiding the whole proceedings. Only arbitration documents shall be applied unless the arbitrator is of the opinion that a hearing is necessary or that the parties agree otherwise.[127] Furthermore, even when hearings are necessary, they may, without limitation, be conducted in person, by video link, by telephone or online (by e-mail or by other electronic or computer communication).[128] A witness may give oral evidence by video link or by telephone or may give written evidence online and be cross-examined thereon.[129]

127. While allowing the adoption of online facilities, the rules provide that the HKIAC shall make all reasonable endeavours to provide security for the transmission of data online between the parties, the arbitrator, Secretary General or his or her designate, and that the HKIAC shall use its best endeavours to see to it that the data is inaccessible or accessible only in an encrypted form to other persons.[130]

128. The timeline of the arbitration procedure is listed as Appendix B, which clearly shows the efficiency of this new procedure. A claimant completes Form N (Notice of Arbitration) and submits it with the appropriate fee to the HKIAC to initiate arbitration. Within fourteen days of receipt of Form N, the respondent shall send the claimant a response as per Form R. The HKIAC shall acknowledge the application, appropriate fee and verifies whether the respondent has a copy of the application within this period.[131] The application to appoint an arbitrator shall be made within forty-two days from the commencement of the arbitration. In case no agreement is reached concerning the arbitrator, the HKIAC shall have the power to appoint an arbitrator upon the application of either party.[132]

129. Within fourteen days of receipt by the claimant of the arbitrator's acceptance of the appointment, the claimant shall submit a Statement of Claim to the

---

126. Article 5 of the Electronic Transactions Arbitration Rules.
127. *Ibid.*, Art. 7(1).
128. *Ibid.*, Art. 9(1).
129. *Ibid.*, Art. 10(5).
130. *Ibid.*, Art. 9(7).
131. *Ibid.*, Art. 1.
132. *Ibid.*, Art. 3.

HKIAC setting out a full description in narrative form of the nature and circumstances of the dispute specifying all factual matters and, if necessary for the proper understanding of the claim, a summary of any contentions of law relied upon and the relief claimed.[133] The same period shall apply to the respondent to submit a Statement of Defence and Counterclaims (if any) upon receipt of the Statement of Claim.[134] The period of fourteen days shall still apply respectively when the claimant wants to send a Statement of Reply and Defence to Counterclaims upon receipt of the Statement of Defence; and when the respondent wants to submit a Statement of Reply regarding Counterclaims (where there is a Defence to Counterclaims).[135]

130. Based on the documents submitted, the arbitrator can decide upon the necessity of hearings, witnesses and assessors. With all the necessary materials, the arbitrator can render an award. The time limit within which the arbitrator must render a final award under the rules is six months from the date the arbitrator is appointed.[136] This period has been rather short compared with other mechanisms.

131. One last thing to note about these rules is that they are not limited to disputes arising out of electronic transactions. Parties who wish to arbitrate their disputes online can refer the dispute to be determined in accordance with these rules regardless of its origin.

§6. Electronic Business Related Arbitration and Mediation

132. Electronic Business Related Arbitration and Mediation (eBRAM) Platform was launched in 2018 to provide an efficient, cost-effective and secure platform for online deal-making and resolving disputes among parties in any part of the world by integrating modern technologies such as blockchain, smart contract and artificial intelligence.[137]

---

133. *Ibid.*, Art. 6(2).
134. *Ibid.*, Art. 6(4).
135. *Ibid.*, Art. 6(6), 6(8).
136. *Ibid.*, Art. 17(5).
137. eBRAM, https://www.doj.gov.hk/en/legal_dispute/online_dispute_resolution_and_lawtech.html.

Part II. Protection of Intellectual Property in the ICT Sector

Chapter 1. Application of Copyright in the Area of ICT

§1. General Introduction

133. Hong Kong has successfully legislated its intellectual property law to ensure strong protection against infringement in any form. Hong Kong has been a member of several important conventions in the world[138] as well as the World Intellectual Property Organization as part of China's delegation.

134. Copyright is a property right subsisting in original literary works (including books and computer software), dramatic, musical or artistic works (including drawings, regardless of artistic merit); sound recordings, films, broadcasts or cable programmes; and the typographical arrangement of published editions.[139] It provides an author with a tool to protect a work from being taken, used and exploited by others without permission. Copyright is held by an author upon a work's creation and fixation in tangible form. Copyright subsists on creation of the work, and there is no need for registration. The duration of copyright for literary, dramatic, musical or artistic works is fifty years from the end of the calendar year in which the author dies. For computer-generated work, the copyright expires fifty years from the calendar year in which the work was made.[140] Hong Kong's Copyright Ordinance (Cap. 528) is the basic document providing protection to copyright. It contains a number of provisions which specifically target the copyright issue regarding the Internet.

§2. Copyright and Its Application Regarding the Internet

135. The general concept of copyright is applicable in the area of ICT. The ordinance provides protection for the following subject matters: published and unpublished original literary, dramatic, musical and artistic works; sound recordings;

138. The Conventions include the Paris Convention for the Protection of Industrial Property, the Bern Convention for the Protection of Literary and Artistic Works, and the Geneva and Paris Universal Copyright Conventions.
139. Section 2 of the Copyright Ordinance.
140. Section 17(2)–(3) of the Copyright Ordinance.

films; broadcasts; cable programmes; published editions.[141] The ordinance protects not only underlying works but also the typographical arrangements of the published editions of literary, dramatic and musical works (including those in which copyright protection is not available for the underlying work).

136. Computer programs are included in literary work; however, no clear definition is offered. To be protected as literary work, computer programs should be in writing. As provided in the ordinance, 'writing' includes any form of notation or code, whether by hand or otherwise and regardless of the method by which, or medium in or on which, it is recorded.[142]

137. No formalities are required to obtain copyright protection for works in Hong Kong. Works of authors from any place in the world, or works first published anywhere in the world, shall be qualified for copyright protection in Hong Kong.

138. The owner of the copyright in a work has the exclusive right in Hong Kong to:

(a) copy the work;
(b) issue copies of the work to the public;
(c) rent copies of the work to the public, (*see* section 25); (Replaced 15 of 2007 section 5);
(d) make available copies of the work to the public;
(e) perform, show or play the work in public;
(f) broadcast the work or include it in a cable programme service;
(g) make an adaptation of the work or do any of the above in relation to an adaptation.[143]

139. The Copyright (Amendment) Ordinance 2007 has partly relaxed the prohibitions against importation and use of parallel imported copies of copyright works by business end-users. Parallel imports of computer software products have been fully liberalized since 2003 and permitted only if the business is the end-user. It does not extend to free use in entirety.[144] The period in relation to which criminal sanctions will arise has also been shortened from eighteen months to fifteen months.[145]

140. The act of uploading a copyrighted work to a website constitutes a reproduction of that work in a material form.[146] Corresponding to such an action, section 205(2) of the ordinance provides that references to the making available to the public of copies of a fixation of a performance are to be made available by wire or by

141. Part II of the Copyright Ordinance.
142. Section 198 of the Copyright Ordinance.
143. Section 22(1) of the Copyright Ordinance.
144. Available at https://www.ipd.gov.hk/eng/intellectual_property/copyright/parallel_imports_leaflet_e.pdf.
145. FAQs on Copyright (Amendment) Ordinance 2007, Intellectual Property Department.
146. Section 26(2) of Copyright Ordinance.

wireless means, in such a way that members of the public in Hong Kong or elsewhere may access the fixation from any place and at any time individually chosen by them (such as the making available of copies of works through the service commonly known as the Internet).[147]

§3. Moral Rights

141. Meanwhile, three types of moral rights are also established in the ordinance: the right to be identified as the author or director of the work (paternity right);[148] the right of the author or director of the work to object to derogatory treatment of the work (integrity right);[149] and the right of everyone not to have work falsely attributed to them (protection against false attribution),[150] which expires twenty years after that person's death.[151] Neither the integrity right[152] nor the paternity right[153] applies to computer programs, design of a typeface or any computer-generated work.

142. The author or director of a copyrighted work has the right to be identified as the author or director of the work. This right may be asserted generally or in relation to any specified act or description of acts.[154] However, this right is subject to several exceptions. One important relevant exception applies to a computer program, the design of a typeface or any computer-generated work.[155] A person does not infringe this right unless there has been an assertion of the right by the author that binds that person. Displaying of a work on the Internet may be considered a public exhibition;[156] for the purpose of assertion, authors should always identify themselves on any copyright works appearing on the Internet.

143. The author or director of a copyrighted work has the right not to have his or her work subjected to derogatory treatment. Such treatment means any addition to, deletion from or alteration to or adaptation of the work, other than a translation of a literary or dramatic work, or an arrangement or transcription of a musical work involving no more than a change of key or register. Derogatory treatment shall amount to distortion or mutilation of the work or is otherwise prejudicial to the honour or reputation of the author or director.[157]

147. Such wording can also be found in s. 26(2) of Copyright Ordinance.
148. Section 89 of the Copyright Ordinance.
149. Section 92 of the Copyright Ordinance.
150. Section 96 of the Copyright Ordinance.
151. Section 97(2) of the Copyright Ordinance.
152. Section 93(2) of the Copyright Ordinance.
153. Section 91(2) of the Copyright Ordinance.
154. Section 90 of the Copyright Ordinance.
155. Section 91(2) of the Copyright Ordinance.
156. Section 90(1) of the Copyright Ordinance.
157. Section 92(2) of the Copyright Ordinance.

144. However, as provided in the Copyright Ordinance, the right to object to derogatory treatment of a work does not apply to a computer program or any computer-generated work.[158] The ordinance further lists the qualification of integrity rights in certain cases in section 94.[159]

145. A person has the right not to have a work falsely attributed to him or her as an author or director. Issuing or making available to the public copies of such a falsely attributed work or public exhibition of a work on which there is a false attribution shall constitute an infringement.[160]

§4. Primary Infringement

146. A copyright is primarily infringed when one of the exclusive rights of the copyright holder is violated. A plaintiff is required to prove ownership of the copyright and copying by the defendant, but proof of intent is not necessary in primary infringement cases. The ordinance sets out several types of actions as primary infringement: the person who carries out such activities shall be liable regardless of whether he or she has the intention or the knowledge. Such activities include copying; issuing copies to the public; making available copies to the public; performance, playing or showing of the work in public; broadcast or inclusion in a cable programme service; making an adaptation or act done in relation to the adaptation.[161] The activities are carried out in relation to the whole or a substantial part of the copyrighted work.[162] According to the ordinance, the action of 'copy' means reproducing the work in any material form, which includes storing the work in any medium by electronic means.[163] The act of making a copyrighted work available over the Internet without permission of the copyright owner shall constitute an infringement of copyright. The act of 'saving' a work from the Internet to a PC constitutes copying. This shall also include storing the work by electronic means or making transient or incidental copies of a work.[164] For example, copies of works made by ISP 'caching' web pages may constitute infringement. However, the ordinance further provides that a transient or incidental copy of a work will not infringe copyright when the person to whom the work was made available in order to view or listen to the work technically requires that copy.[165]

158. Section 93(2) of the Copyright Ordinance.
159. For example, s. 94 applies to: (a) works in which copyright originally vested in the author's employer in the course of employment; (b) works in which government copyright or Legislative Council copyright subsists; (c) works in which copyright originally vested in an international organization.
160. Section 96(2) of the Copyright Ordinance.
161. Sections 23–29 of the Copyright Ordinance.
162. *Chow Wai Man, Vivian & Polygram Records Ltd. v. Easy Finder Ltd.*, HCA No. 4042 of 1995.
163. Section 23(2) of the Copyright Ordinance.
164. Section 23(6) of the Copyright Ordinance.
165. Section 65 of the Copyright Ordinance.

§5. Secondary Infringement

147. This type of infringement differs from primary infringement in that the intention or knowledge of the party is a vital element in deciding liability. Liability may be imposed on persons who have not personally engaged in the infringing activities, but where it may appear that one individual should be held accountable for the actions of another. In this situation, substantial or persuasive involvement of the infringer is required. The alleged infringer must have knowledge or reason to believe that his or her activity would infringe copyright.[166] Copyright in a work is infringed by a person who, without the licence of the copyright owner – (a) makes; (b) imports into Hong Kong or exports from Hong Kong; (c) possesses for the purpose of or in the course of any trade or business; or (Amended 64 of 2000 section 3; 15 of 2007 section 8); (d)sells or lets for hire, or offers or exposes for sale or hire.[167]

148. The most relevant provision here has been section 32(2) on providing means for making infringing copies: copyright in a work is infringed by a person who, without the licence of the copyright owner, transmits the work by means of a telecommunications system (other than broadcasting or including the work in a cable programme service), knowing or having reason to believe that infringing copies of the work will be made of the reception of the transmission in Hong Kong or elsewhere. A telecommunications system is defined as a system for transmitting visual images, sounds or other information by electronic means.[168]

149. Thus, the Internet is obviously included in this section. The Copyright Ordinance has also defined the term 'infringing copy' as follows:

A copy of a work other than a copy of an accessory work is an infringing copy if:

(a) it has been or is proposed to be imported into Hong Kong; and
(b) its production in Hong Kong would have constituted an infringement of the copyright in the work in question or a breach of an exclusive licence agreement relating to that work.[169]

§6. Infringement on the Internet

150. Downloading a file from an Internet site onto a viewer's hard disk without permission, express or implied, constitutes the making of an unauthorized copy in violation of the exclusive right of the copyright owner as long as the originality is satisfied. Thus, one is required to have either an assignment of the copyright or a

166. *CBS Songs Ltd. & Others v. Amstrad Consumer Electronics Plc. & Another* [1988] AC 1013.
167. Sections 30–34 of the Copyright Ordinance.
168. Section 198(1) of the Copyright Ordinance.
169. Section 35(3) of the Copyright Ordinance.

licence to use the material. One's further action of uploading a copyrighted work to a web constitutes reproduction of that work in a material form.

151. Sending unauthorized copies of copyrighted works via e-mail may result in liability to both sender and recipient, as well as the online system on which the e-mail is stored.

152. Posting messages to private online services and Internet newsgroups – where such posting exhibits the originality sufficient to trigger copyright protection – constitutes infringement since it causes the message to be copied and stored on computers across the world for their subscribers to view.

153. A hyperlink is an element in an electronic document that links to another place in the same document or to an entirely different document, which can enable users to jump from one Internet site to another. A hyperlink is not a cable programme as defined in the Copyright Ordinance. A cable programme service is a service for making available to the public copies of works or fixations of performances but excluding a service in which the transmission of moving visual representational images is an essential feature (such as the service commonly known as video-on-demand).[170]

154. Generally speaking, a licence is implied since the act of implementing and maintaining a public access website grants an implicit licence to enter and explore. Another reason for infringement exemption may be that it is not a 'reproduction' because of its temporary nature as defined in the Copyright Ordinance, 'copyright in a work is not infringed by the making of a transient and incidental copy which is technically required for the viewing or listening of the work by a member of the public to whom a copy of the work is made available'.[171] Accordingly, short pieces of text, such as titles of web pages or hyperlinked texts, may not have the requisite degree of originality to constitute infringement.[172]

155. However, if a hyperlink misleads commercial connection between the site containing the link and the site on which the work is located, there might be an infringement. Also, if such a hyperlink can produce confusion concerning the author of the site linked, this could lead to infringement of false attribution.

§7. Copyright (Amendment) Ordinance

156. The Copyright (Amendment) Ordinance 2007 introduces a number of new civil and criminal liabilities:[173]

170. Section 9(2) of the Copyright Ordinance.
171. Section 65 of the Copyright Ordinance.
172. *Exxon Corp. v. Exxon Insurance Consultants* [1981] 3 ALL ER 241.
173. FAQs on Amendments to the Copyright Ordinance (2007–2009), Intellectual Property Department.

(a) a new business end-user criminal offence against the infringing acts of making with a view to distributing or distributing infringing copies of copyright works published in four types of printed works, namely newspapers, magazines, periodicals and books (the 'copying and distribution offence');
(b) a new criminal offence that may be applicable to the director(s), partner(s) or persons(s) responsible for the internal management of a body corporate or partnership if the body corporate or partnership is found to have committed an act which attracts one of the aforesaid business end-user criminal liabilities, unless he or she proves that he or she did not authorize such act;
(c) a new criminal offence against any person who is engaged in commercial dealing of circumvention tools or provides circumvention services on a commercial basis for the circumvention of technological measures (i.e., access control measures or copy-protection measures);
(d) extended civil liability against any person who deals in circumvention tools or provides circumvention services (whether or not in a commercial context) for the circumvention of technological measures;
(e) new civil liability against any person who circumvents a technological measure used for copyright protection.

The copying and distribution offence will also apply to distribution of digital copies through any electronic medium. The Copyright (Amendment) Ordinance 2009 prescribes two separate sets of numeric limits within which the copying and distribution offence does not apply.

Chapter 2. Legal Protection of Software

157. The computer software industry is widely recognized as an engine of economic development and growth in a modern economy. This is also the case in Hong Kong. The computer software industry in Hong Kong stimulated growth through the creation of highly skilled and highly paid jobs, substantial tax revenues, and the development of tools needed to enable local industries to compete effectively in the global market.[174] In Hong Kong, a computer program is not patentable if it produces a result which is not new.[175]

158. Software piracy is a serious problem facing the Hong Kong market. The rate of software piracy in Hong Kong was estimated to have been 64% in 1996 (and declined to only 45% in 2010), resulting in USD 129 million in direct revenue losses to the local industry.[176] The low prices fuelled high demand; the pirated copies exist throughout all segments of society.[177]

159. The Hong Kong Government set out to fight software piracy. Significant steps have been taken to better protect intellectual property rights in Hong Kong. The Customs and Excise Department, containing a special intellectual property rights unit with a 147-member Special Task Force, has also taken strict measures against retail shops selling pirated goods under the title of copyright infringement. The HKSAR Government has further instituted a licensing regime for the import and export of production equipment and has passed a law that requires factories to register and use source identifier codes. The issue of licensing can become more difficult when an implied licence is claimed. Such a licence can arise out of a course of dealings or to give business efficacy to certain arrangements.[178]

160. The Prevention of Copyright Piracy Ordinance (Cap. 544) established a licensing regime to prevent piracy. The Commissioner of Customs and Excise and any Deputy or Assistant Commissioner of Customs and Excise have the authority to issue a licence for the present purpose. Only those holding a valid licence have the right to manufacture the optical discs, with the exception of an employee of a licensee who manufactures in the course of his or her employment or manufactures for the purpose prescribed by relevant regulations.[179] The manufacturing of the optical discs can only take place on the licensed premises.

161. In granting a licence, the Commissioner:

(a) shall assign to the licensee a manufacturer's code;

174. P. Lovelock, *Fighting 21st Century Pirates: The Business Software Alliance in Hong Kong*, Centre for Asian Business Cases 2 (U.H.K. 1999).
175. Section 93(3) of the Patent Ordinance (Cap. 514).
176. BSA and Software Publishers Association (SPA), Contribution of the Packaged Software Industry to the Hong Kong Economy, May 1998.
177. D.E. Sanger, *In Pact with China, a Ghost of Japan* (N.Y. Times 27 Feb. 1995).
178. *See*, e.g., *Saphena Computing Ltd. v. Allied Collection Agencies Ltd.* [1995] FSR 616.
179. Section 3 of the Prevention of Copyright Piracy Ordinance.

(b) shall impose all of the conditions as may be published by him or her from time to time by notice in the *Gazette* for the purpose of this section; and
(c) may impose such other conditions as he or she thinks fit for:
  (i) preventing the manufacture of infringing copies of copyright works;
  (ii) protecting the rights of copyright owners and other persons to whom rights are conferred under the Copyright Ordinance (Cap. 528);
  (iii) securing compliance by the licensee with any provisions of this Part or any regulations made for the purposes of this Part;
  (iv) securing compliance by the licensee with any conditions of the licence; and
  (v) ensuring the effective administration of this Part.[180]

162. A manufacturer's code shall consist of:

(a) one or more letters or numbers;
(b) a mark, sign, symbol or device; or
(c) any combination of letters, numbers, marks, signs, symbols or devices, as determined by the Commissioner.[181]

163. The ordinance further regulates transfer, display, revocation or cancellation of the licence, which formulates a complete licensing regime for optical disc manufacturing. Nevertheless, it is noted that three exceptions have been provided in the Copyright Ordinance permitting legitimate copying of software, the purpose of which is to allow corrections of software malfunctions and to use and protect the software in the normal course of operation. The three exceptions are:

(a) a lawful user may make a back-up copy for his or her lawful use;[182]
(b) a lawful user may copy or adapt the program if the copying or adapting is necessary for his or her lawful use;[183] and
(c) a lawful user may, in particular if it is necessary for the lawful use of the program, copy the program or adapt it for the purpose of correcting errors therein.[184]

164. Reverse engineering is a method of reconstructing a computer model from a physical object through dimensional measurement and surface modelling. Can developers disassemble and recompile a program and use what they have learned to create an interoperable or competing program? According to the second and third exceptions listed above, it might be the case that the owner of the copyright in the computer program will want to reserve to himself or herself the right to make

180. Section 5(2) of the Prevention of Copyright Piracy Ordinance.
181. Section 5(3) of the Prevention of Copyright Piracy Ordinance.
182. Section 60(1) of the Copyright Ordinance.
183. Section 61(1) of the Copyright Ordinance.
184. Section 61(2) of the Copyright Ordinance.

the adaptation, even for the purpose of correcting errors so that any adaptation that is necessary is carried out to the standards the copyright owner would like to see implemented.[185]

185. P. Stephenson, et al., *Cyberlaw in Hong Kong* 178–180 (2d ed. Lexis Nexis 2007).

Chapter 3. Legal Protection of Databases

165. The separate items in the database can be literary works, artistic works or non-works, which are protected by the Copyright Ordinance. Other elements of the database, however, can also be protected under the same ordinance as a compilation. The ordinance provides that 'literary work' means any work, other than a dramatic or musical work, which is written, spoken or sung, and includes a compilation of data or other material in any form which, by reason of the selection or arrangement of its contents, constitutes an intellectual creation, including but not limited to a table.[186]

166. Databases are protected against misappropriation by third parties, including competitors. Websites may contain secrets in the form of data on log files and information obtained from an audit of what visitors do at a corporate website. For this purpose, databases can be protected as trade secrets. Companies can use encryption and other information security tools to maintain the secrecy of information. If a website developer is building a specialized company database, corporate counsel may wish to draft non-competition and non-disclosure agreements.

167. The Prevention of Copyright Piracy Ordinance is also relevant in the protection of databases. As defined by the ordinance, 'optical disc' includes any other medium or device on which data may be stored in digital form and be read by means of a laser, and, for greater certainty, includes any such medium or device manufactured for any purpose, whether or not any data readable by means of a laser has been stored thereon. Thus, the licensing regime established also applies in the present situation.[187] Only those holding a valid licence have the right to manufacture the optical discs: constructing databases for commercial purposes.

186. Section 4(1)(a) of the Copyright Ordinance.
187. Section 2 of the Prevention of Copyright Piracy Ordinance.

Chapter 4. Legal Protection of Computer Chips

168. Computer chips, such as integrated circuits, are protected by intellectual property rights. Protection for these products is available under the Layout-Design (Topography) of Integrated Circuits Ordinance (Cap. 445), which recognizes and protects rights in works affixed in semiconductor chip products for a period of ten years following the date of first commercial exploitation.[188]

169. According to the ordinance, commercial exploitation includes, by way of trade:

(a) to sell, let for hire or otherwise dispose of;
(b) to offer or expose for sale or hire or otherwise offer to dispose of or expose for the purpose of disposing of; or
(c) to import for the purpose of sale, letting for hire or other disposition.[189]

170. A layout-design (topography) owned by a qualified owner shall be protected as long as it is original in the sense that it is the result of its creator's own intellectual effort and is not commonplace among creators of layout-designs (topographies) and manufacturers of integrated circuits at the time of its creations; or in the case of a layout-design (topography) that consists of a combination of elements and interconnections that are commonplace, the combination, taken as a whole, is original in the sense that it is the result of its creator's own intellectual effort and is not commonplace among creators of layout-designs (topographies) and manufacturers of integrated circuits at the time of its creation.[190]

171. Subject to certain exceptions, the owner is able to take civil action to prohibit others from reproducing or distributing his or her layout-design without his or her consent or without payment of royalties. There is no need to register the layout-design right and protection will be automatic.

172. The qualified owner enjoys the right to reproduce, whether by incorporation into an integrated circuit or otherwise, all or part of his or her protected layout-design (topography) or to commercially exploit his or her protected layout-design (topography), an integrated circuit in which his or her protected layout-design (topography) is incorporated or an article that contains an integrated circuit in which his or her protected layout-design (topography) is incorporated. Any other person who performs the above acts shall be deemed as having infringed a qualified owner's right.[191]

188. D.G. Smith, *Due Diligence in Technology Transaction* (Legal, 21 Dec. 2000–Jan. 2001 GC.comm).
189. Section 2 of the Layout-Design (Topography) of Integrated Circuits Ordinance.
190. Section 3(1) of the Layout-Design (Topography) of Integrated Circuits Ordinance.
191. Section 4 of the Layout-Design (Topography) of Integrated Circuits Ordinance.

Chapter 5. Other Intellectual Property Rights in the ICT Sector

§1. Trademark Protection

173. A trademark is, in essence, a word/picture/logo/three-dimensional object which is used by a trader to denote the origin of a product. It identifies and distinguishes the source of a good or service, protecting words, symbols, slogans, designs, characters, packaging, sounds, smells and colours, as well as product configurations as used in commerce.[192] Distinctiveness is a key element for the protection of a trademark.

174. It must not be descriptive for the goods or services or a characteristic of the goods or services. It may not be a geographical name or deceptive and may not be the same as or confusingly similar to an existing trademark used/registered for the same or similar goods or services. Registered trademarks grant to the owner of the mark the exclusive right to use the mark for the goods or services covered by the specification of the registration.

175. An unregistered trademark may be protected if it can be shown that:

(a) the mark has a reputation established by use;
(b) the defendant is misrepresenting his or her goods or services as those of the plaintiff;
(c) damage has been caused to the plaintiff: loss of profit or loss of reputation.

176. The Trademark Ordinance (Cap. 559) is the primary legislation offering protection for trademarks, effective as of early 2003, which takes into account technological development and simplifies the application and examination procedures. The range of marks which are registrable as trademarks has broadened, for example, by allowing sound and scent to be registered. Assignment and licensing procedures have been simplified, and multi-class applications are allowed.

177. Normally an applicant for a new trademark will be told within about ten months that he or she may advertise his or her proposed mark, provided the criteria laid out in the Trademark Ordinance are met. The public then has a period of two months to object if they have lawful grounds for doing so. Where no objection is received, the mark can normally be registered in a further two months. The whole registration procedure takes about fourteen months if there is no opposition to the mark. The registration is effective from the date of receipt of the valid application by the registry.

178. The ordinance provides protection to registered trademarks and also well-known trademarks.[193] It prevents competitors from free-riding on their rivals' marks

192. Section 3 of the Trademark Ordinance.
193. Section 4 of the Trademark Ordinance.

and capitalizing on their rivals' investment of time, money and resources. Infringement may be based on the simultaneous use of two trademarks likely to cause confusion or dilution. Section 18(1)–(4) specifies the infringing acts for trademarks.

179. In Hong Kong, quite a lot of trademark usage is in Chinese. It is important to advertise goods or services in Chinese marks in Hong Kong. Chinese character marks are registrable under the ordinance, though there is no requirement for a trademark owner to register the Chinese character version of his or her mark. Mere registration of the English version of the trademark does not protect the Chinese counterpart.

180. To prove trademark infringement, a trademark owner must prove that the competing use of the mark is capable of generating a likelihood of confusion concerning the source of its product or that there are forms of dilution.

181. The Trade Descriptions Ordinance (Cap. 362) prohibits the use of false trade description with regard to the sale, import or export of goods in Hong Kong.[194] A 'false trade description' also includes the use of a forged trademark or a mark so nearly resembling a trademark as to be calculated to deceive. Anyone who applies a forged trademark or a mark so nearly resembling a trademark as to be calculated to deceive to goods; sells or offers those goods for sale; possesses those goods for the purposes of trade or manufacture shall be deemed to have committed an offence.[195]

182. The Internet raises challenging issues for trademark law. When displaying a trademark on the website, one must obtain the permission of the owner. One cannot advertise goods or services using the same or a similar trademark causing damage to the owner of the trademark. The way of defining infringement shall still apply the traditional means. In hyperlinking, the owner of a trademark logo can object to the placement of that logo on one's website without permission. The use of a logo as a hyperlink to another website could give rise to copyright infringement, but not if a plain word trademark is used. Any company operating a website needs to understand how trademark law impacts their choice of a domain name, their development of a brand, and their relations with competitors, 'cybersquatters' or other entities who want to exploit their name. It is to be noted that the two are distinct; securing a trademark over a name does not automatically grant an exclusive right/ownership over the domain name, and vice versa.

§2. Patent Infringement

183. Patents, property rights possessed or held by an inventor, are granted for inventions fulfilling the conditions of novelty, utility and non-obviousness. A patent can protect products and software. There are three types of patents: utility patents,

194. Section 7 of the Trade Description Ordinance.
195. Section 9(1)–9(2) of the Trade Description Ordinance.

design patents and plant patents. Since the emergence of e-commerce, new terms have appeared, such as e-commerce patents, Internet process patents and business method patents. Software, which produces a technical effect, is frequently classified as a utility patent and may encompass long-distance communication networks, voice, video and data communication as well as Internet-related business methods.

184. Hong Kong does not have its own patent examination facilities but instead re-registers patents registered in other designated patent offices.[196] However, the Hong Kong courts have the power to revoke patents on the application of any person on certain grounds.[197]

185. The Patents Ordinance (Cap. 514) offers the criteria for deciding on patentability. The basic standard is that an invention is patentable if it is susceptible to industrial application, is new and involves an inventive step. However, a discovery, scientific theory or mathematical method, or an aesthetic creation, or a scheme, rule or method for performing a mental act, playing a game or doing business, or a program for a computer, or the presentation of information shall be excluded from the scope of inventions as far as a patent or patent application relates to such subject matter or activities as such.[198]

186. Standard patents in the HKSAR have a term of protection of up to twenty years. Patentability of standard patents and their application is further defined in Patent (General) Rules.[199] Applicants seeking protection of a standard patent must make an application to the HKSAR Patents Registry within six months after the date of publication of their patent application at the Chinese, European or United Kingdom Patent Office.

187. The so-called short-term patent with a short commercial viability shall enjoy protection for eight years. Applications are made directly to the HKSAR Patents Registry and are granted subject to a formality examination. Short-term patent applications in the HKSAR can enjoy Paris Convention priority. According to this convention, any person who has duly filed an application for a patent in one of the Member States of the convention shall enjoy, for the purpose of filing in the other Member States, a right of priority for a period of twelve months, which starts from the date of filing of the first application.[200]

188. The Patents Ordinance offers protection to the patent owner. It allows for the grant of an independent patent in Hong Kong based on the patents granted by the United Kingdom being independent and would be capable of being tested for validity, rectified, amended, revoked and enforced in Hong Kong.

---

196. The designated patent offices are those of Mainland China, the United Kingdom and the European Patent Office.
197. Section 91(1) of the Patents Ordinance.
198. Section 93(1)–(3) of the Patents Ordinance.
199. Available at https://www.elegislation.gov.hk/hk/cap514C?xpid=ID_1573438607512_001.
200. Article 4 of the Paris Convention for the Protection of Industrial Property, of 20 Mar. 1883, as amended on 28 Sep. 1979.

189. A direct infringer is a person or entity that does not have a licence or other authority to use an invention but who nevertheless uses, offers to sell or sells any patented invention during the patent term. The ordinance prevents direct use of the invention in force by persons other than its proprietor.

190. Such uses include the following:

(a) in relation to any product which is the subject matter of the patent, making, putting on the market, using or importing the product; or stocking the product, whether for the purpose of putting it on the market or otherwise;
(b) in relation to any process which is the subject matter of the patent, using the process or offering the process for use in Hong Kong when the third party knows, or it is obvious to a reasonable person in the circumstances, that the use of the process is prohibited without the consent of the proprietor of the patent;
(c) where the invention is a process, then in relation to any product obtained directly by means of that process, putting on the market, using or importing the product, or stocking the product, whether for the purpose of putting it on the market or otherwise.[201]

191. An indirect infringer is a person or entity that actively encourages another person or entity to infringe a patented invention. All third parties without the consent of the patent proprietor shall be prevented from indirect use of the invention, with means relating to an essential element of that invention, for putting it into effect, when the third party knows, or it is obvious in the circumstances to a reasonable person, that the said means are suitable and intended for putting that invention into effect in Hong Kong.

§3. Registered Design Rights

192. 'Design' means features of shape, configuration, pattern or ornament applied to an article by any industrial process, being features which in the finished article appeal to and are judged by the eye but do not include a method or principle of construction or features of shape or configuration of an article which are dictated solely by the function which the article has to perform or are dependent upon the appearance of another article of which the article is intended by the designer to form an integral part.[202]

193. The Registered Designs Ordinance offers the framework for protection. Applicants can apply for registration of designs directly with the Hong Kong Designs Registry. Designs are subjected to a formality examination before registration. To be registered, a design must be new. The system requires no substantive examination. It is to be noted that a computer program, a protected layout-design

201. Section 73 of the Patents Ordinance.
202. Section 2(1) of the Registered Designs Ordinance (Cap. 522).

(topography), cannot be registered as a design.[203] It only protects the outward appearance of new three-dimensional objects which have aesthetic appeal.

194. Section 31(1) confers the registered owner the exclusive rights to make in Hong Kong or import into Hong Kong for sale or hire, or for use for the purpose of trade or business; or to sell, hire, or offer or expose for sale or hire in Hong Kong, any article in respect of which the design is registered and to which that design or a design not substantially different from it has been applied. Accordingly, when carrying out e-commerce, the importer has to be careful to determine whether the products violate the ordinance.

§4. Trade Secret

195. No specific ordinance exists in Hong Kong covering trade secrets. However, some relevant provisions can be found in the Trade Description Ordinance (Cap. 362). According to section 2 of the ordinance, 'trade description' includes an indication, direct or indirect, and by whatever means given, of any of the following matters with respect to any goods or parts of goods, that is to say:

(a) quantity (which includes length, width, height, area, volume, capacity, weight and number), size or gauge;
(b) method of manufacture, production, processing or reconditioning;
(c) composition;
(d) fitness for purpose, strength, performance, behaviour or accuracy;
(e) any physical characteristics not included in the preceding paragraphs;
(f) testing by any person and results thereof;
(g) approval by any person or conformity with a type approved by any person;
(h) place or date of manufacture, production, processing or reconditioning;
(i) person by whom manufactured, produced, processed or reconditioned;
(j) other history, including previous ownership or use.

196. Thus, trade secrets can be implied in any of the above categories. The ordinance further prohibits the illegal disclosure of trade secrets obtained by him or her in premises, which he or she has entered, to any other person unless such disclosure was made under a court order or for the purpose of performing functions under this ordinance.[204] Such disclosure can constitute an offence. False trade descriptions, forged trademarks and misstatements in respect of goods supplied in the course of trade are also prohibited by the ordinance: any person who disposes of or has in his or her possession any die, block, machine or other instruments for the purpose of making, or applying to goods, a false trade description commits an offence unless he or she proves that he or she acted without intent to defraud.[205]

203. Section 8 of the Registered Design Ordinance.
204. Section 17(2) of the Trade Description Ordinance.
205. Section 7 of the Trade Description Ordinance.

Chapter 6. Internet Domain Name Registration

§1. General Introduction

197. Every computer that is Internet-enabled will have both an Internet Protocol (IP) address and a domain name. An IP is a numeric address given to each computer, server, workstation or other equipment that is connected to the Internet. The IP addresses consist of four sets of numbers each between 1 and 255. Since it is very difficult to remember such numerical IP addresses, a domain name system was established. Thus, the domain name system was initially established to help identify a specific website. One advantage to registering a distinctive domain name is that consumers tend to guess when trying to find a particular company's website.

198. The best domain names are easy to remember and help brand a company's products or services. People can analyse a domain name and learn something about the host computer or its owner. Thus, companies pay much attention to the registration of the appropriate domain name, as failure to procure the proper identity may result in a loss of potential customers, business partners or other opportunities. Company websites need to register their domain names with one of the ICANN-accredited registrars. The ICANN was created as a non-profit public sector corporation to serve the operational standards of the Internet.

199. Generally, when registering, applicants must produce evidence that:

(a) the registration is complete and accurate;
(b) the domain name does not infringe trademarks of third parties;
(c) the domain name is not registered for unlawful purposes;
(d) the domain name owner will not knowingly use the domain name to violate any laws or regulations.

200. Domain names are hierarchical and consist of two levels: Top-Level Domain (TLD) and Second-Level Domain (SLD). There are two types of TLDs: generic TLDs (gTLDs) and country-code TLDs (ccTLDs). Formerly there were seven gTLDs, but now additional suffixes have been added. Nearly every country in the world now has ccTLDs, and each has its own variation on the accepted naming convention with two characters representing the country of origin. The domain name '.hk' is allocated for Hong Kong.

§2. Registration in Hong Kong

201. Formerly, the Hong Kong Network Information Centre was in charge of domain name registration in Hong Kong. It operated under the auspices of the Joint Universities Computer Centre (JUCC). An inauguration ceremony of the Hong Kong Internet Registration Corporation Limited (HKIRC) on 22 April 2002 marked the successful completion of the transfer of the domain name administration functions from the JUCC to the HKIRC, which is a non-profit, non-statutory corporation responsible for the administration of Internet domain names under '.hk' country-code TLD since that date.

202. The government endorsed the application of the HKIRC to the ICANN for ICANN's re-delegation to administer '.hk' domain name registration in Hong Kong. The tripartite relationship among the ICANN, the government and the HKIRC has been set out in a Memorandum of Understanding signed by the HKIRC and the government. The HKIRC provides registration services through its wholly-owned subsidiary, HKDNR, for domain names ending with 'com.hk', 'org.hk', 'gov.hk', 'edu.hk' and 'net.hk',[206] and any other SLDs to be introduced.

203. The HKIRC announced in December 2009 that '.' registrations will be offered free to all '.hk' customers in the second half of 2010 with the aim of helping them develop their sites with full Chinese domain names. This is to increase the popularity of Chinese domain names and to maximize benefits to the Internet community, and ultimately to sustain the status of Hong Kong as a digital city.[207] In January 2014,[208] HKIRC introduced a registry lock service for '.hk'/ ' ... ' domain names called '.hk LOCK' to fight 'domain hijacking' including website defacement, revenue loss or disruption to operations, and confidential information leakage of Internet users. The .hk LOCK service will lock the domain names of users 'against any changes of name server information on the system' and applies '2-step verification process commonly employed by Internet banking'.[209]

204. The HKDNR will not scrutinize applications for domain names, other than in respect of technical restrictions and application qualifications. It will also not make judgments as to whether the registration or use of a domain name infringes the rights of any third parties.

§3. Registration Rules

205. To qualify for registration, an applicant must be one of the following legal entities in Hong Kong: a commercial entity (.com.hk), a non-profitable organization (.org.hk), an entity managing network infrastructure and services (.net.hk), a bureau or department of the HKSAR Government (.gov.hk) or educational institution (.edu.hk). To prove its physical presence in Hong Kong, the applicants are required to show evidence of a relevant registration document, such as the Business Registration Certificate. The application for and any subsequent registration of a Chinese

206. HKIRC, at www.hkdnr.net.hk.
207. HKIRC to launch '.' full Chinese domain name in 2010 Available free to '.hk' corporations and users and further upholding the status of Hong Kong as a leading digital city, 21 Dec. 2009 (available at https://www.hkirc.hk/content.jsp?id=63#!/&in=/company_info/pressrelease.jsp?item=193).
208. HKIRC 2013–2014 Annual Report (available at https://www.hkirc.hk/pdf/general_meetings/agm/2014/Annual_Report/v_New%20Services%20and%20Development.pdf).
209. Available at https://www.hkirc.hk/useHKLock/index.html.

domain name is deemed to include all possible combinations of the Chinese domain name using different Chinese character variants (in the same sequential order as the order designated in the application). This is so even though only the Chinese domain name is actually applied (including the all-traditional and all-simplified Chinese versions of the Chinese domain name), and none of its other different Chinese character variants may be activated for use.[210]

206. Individuals were not allowed to register domain names before 21 February 2003. However, a new domain name for individuals (idv.hk) was launched by that date. All Hong Kong ID cardholders aged 11 or above (parents/guardians shall jointly apply for registrants from age 11 through 18) may apply for their exclusive domain names ending with '.hk'.

207. The same entity can register for more than one domain name, and domain names can be transferred from one entity to another entity of the same type, as long as the recipient can also show a valid presence in Hong Kong.

208. The applicant can fill in the online application form at the HKDNR website. An agent, such as an ISP, can undertake the application process on behalf of the applicant. However, the applicant should make sure that its Business Registration Certificate is used and its e-mail address is listed as the Administrative Contact.

209. Subject to the Soft Launch Period Rules, domain names are registered on a first-come, first-served basis. To register the name, the applicant must have a bona fide intention to use a name on a regular basis on the Internet. Failure to do so for a period of ninety days or more may result in deregistration of the domain name. The applicant must warrant that the use of the registration of the name does not interfere with or infringe the right of any third party in any jurisdiction with respect to trademark, service mark, trade name, company name or any other intellectual property rights.

210. To register an '.hk' domain name, the applicant needs to first check for the availability of the domain name and prepare the relevant documentary proof of the Business Registration Certificate. Such an examination ensures that there is no previous registration of the same domain name. The online registration process is available at the website of the HKDNR.[211]

211. Registration processing time will depend on two factors: application action and verification action. Once the online application has been submitted, the HKDNR shall process the registration upon receipt of a copy of documentary proof and the applicable registration fee. After all required documents and fees have been received and verified, a successful e-mail notification will be sent out within three working days. However, if the required documents and payment are not received,

---

210. Article 5.1 of the Hong Kong Domain Name Registration Company Limited Rules for.hk Domain and sub-domains, Version 5.0, effective 25 Feb. 2008.

211. *See* www.hkdnr.net.hk.

an e-mail reminder will be sent out on the fourteenth day from receipt of the application notifying the applicant of the outstanding items. If all the requirements are still not received within the next three subsequent days, the registration will be cancelled.

212. Registration must be renewed annually, and the registrant has the responsibility to keep the information supplied up-to-date.

213. The registration fee for a one-year contract is HKD 200 (HKD 150 for '.idv.hk'; HKD 250 for '.hk'). A Hong Kong ISP can arrange registration for a small administrative fee. The HKDNR is a non-profit company and pays no dividends to its shareholders. The fees charged are to cover the operational costs, which shall be subjected to periodical review. It will employ the latest technology to deliver cost-effective service to its customers.

§4. Combating Cybersquatting

214. As a result of the potential profits of domain names, illegal activities in this sector have also surfaced. Cybersquatting has been so far the most prevalent one. The policy of first-come, first-served allows a registrant to register any desired name as long as it is available at the time of registration. Consequently, nothing guarantees that a trademark owner will be able to register the desired domain name for business. Cybersquatting refers to the activity of registering domain names in bad faith for making profits. Such a domain name has nothing to do with the registrant, who does not intend to make commercial use of the name; the purpose of such a registration is to register and sell. The most common form of cybersquatting is the abusive practice of registering domain names of famous companies and seeking to sell their names back for a profit. The plaintiff can bring an action for trademark infringement or passing off in the courts.[212] It is essential for a plaintiff to show that:

(a) it has acquired a goodwill or reputation attached to the goods or services which it supplies in the mind of the purchasing public by association with the identifying characteristics;
(b) the defendant misrepresents to the public, whether intentionally or not, that goods or services offered by the defendant are the goods or services of the plaintiff; and
(c) damage is suffered or likely to be suffered by reason of such misrepresentation.[213]

215. To combat such activities, the ICANN has formulated new policies for resolving such disputes. Hong Kong has also taken an active attitude in providing

212. *Sun Microsystems v. Lai Sun Hotels* [2000] 2 HKLRD 616.
213. *Reckitt & Colman Products Ltd. v. Borden Inc. & Others* [1990] ALL ER 873.

dispute resolution services through the HKIAC.[214] The HKIRC has introduced a service by using .hk WATCH, which can help to monitor the registration of .hk domain names and have an alert sent to notify a trademark owner if there is a newly registered domain name which may potentially confuse or mislead the targeted audience. This service will help to reduce the possibility of malicious registration and use of .hk domain names in bad faith and potential brand infringement.

214. *See*, e.g., the case of *Lycos*, HKIAC Arbitration Panel Decision 0107-0002.

Part III. ICT Contracts

Chapter 1. Hardware Contracts

216. Hardware suppliers in Hong Kong include International Business Machines (IBM), Compaq, Hewlett Packard and Sun Microsystems. Compaq and IBM dominated the market in the mid-1990s. HP and Compaq merged in 2002. Key developments in recent years have been the battle for the top spot between Dell and HP, and between Lenovo and HP as of 2021.[215]

217. Content owners need to ensure that manufacturers of hardware who present their digital works are consistent with and do not circumvent any content protection technologies they use with their works. They can prevent any hardware manufacturers from making or dealing in hardware that circumvents their content protection measures. This is provided in the Copyright Ordinance concerning devices designed to circumvent copyright protection. As defined, this shall include any device or means specifically intended to prevent or restrict copying of a work or fixation of a performance or to impair the quality of copies or fixations made.[216]

218. The Copyright Ordinance further rules on rights and remedies in respect of unlawful acts that interfere with rights management information. According to the ordinance, rights management information means:

(a) information which identifies the work, the author of the work, the owner of any right in the work, the performer or the performance of the performer;
(b) information about the terms and conditions of use of the work, the person having fixation rights in relation to the performance or the performance; or
(c) any number of codes that represent such information when any of these items of information is attached to a copy of a work or a fixed performance or appears in connection with the making available of a work or a fixed performance to the public.[217]

215. Market share of leading PC vendors (available at http://en.wikipedia.org/wiki/Market_share_of_leading_PC_vendors).
216. Section 273(1) of the Copyright Ordinance.
217. Section 274 of the Copyright Ordinance.

This definition clearly applies to hardware. Hardware contracts should thus be reached taking into account all of these provisions. Further reference can also be made to laws on protection of intellectual property rights as discussed above in Part II.

Chapter 2. Software Contracts

219. The software industry is a key component of the IT services sector. Most of the local software companies in Hong Kong are small firms with less than twenty employees, but it is those companies that provide competitive customized software to support local and foreign customers. According to the Hong Kong Productivity Council, total revenue generated by independent software vendors (twenty-four vendors as of 2021) in Hong Kong amounted to HKD 9 billion in 2000, around 20% of which were export earnings (*see* Table 6).

Table 6 Exports of Computer Software (HKD Million)[218]

	2017	*2018*	*2019*	*2020*
Total Exports	8,040	7,602	5,207	6,309

220. Local dealers are growing in terms of size, scope of operation and sophistication. The Copyright Ordinance treats a computer program and 'preparatory material for a computer program' as a type of literary work.[219] To enjoy copyright protection, the computer program must be original.[220] Satisfying the requirement of originality, the protection of this program starts from the time it is recorded in writing or otherwise.[221] Anyone that violates the rights of the software owner shall be liable. Accordingly, most software contracts involve the protection of software based on copyright. In order to generate sales of a product either online or offline, the copyright owner may allow visitors to access a part of a work so as to entice them to buy the entire work.

221. Once a valid software contract exists, a lawful user of a copy of a computer program may make a back-up copy of the program without infringing the copyright in the program if it is necessary for him or her to have the back-up copy for the purposes of his or her lawful use.[222] Here 'a lawful user' refers to the one with a contractual right to use the program.[223] But this right to a back-up copy can be excluded by the contract.[224] The Copyright Ordinance further provides that a lawful user may copy or adapt the program without infringing the copyright in the

218. *Source: Statistical Digest of the Services Sector*, Census & Statistics Department, May 2016 (available at http://www.statistics.gov.hk/pub/B10800072016AN16B0100.pdf).
Note: Starting from 2007, trade statistics on computer software include imports and exports of recorded magnetic tapes of a width not exceeding 6.5 mm; other optical media and other media for the recording of sound or of other phenomena.
219. Section 4(1)(b) and (c) of the Copyright Ordinance (Cap. 528). *See also Ladbroke (Football) Ltd. v. William Hill (Football) Ltd.* [1964] 1 ALL ER 465.
220. Section 2(1)(a) of the Copyright Ordinance.
221. Section 4(2) of the Copyright Ordinance.
222. Section 60(1) of the Copyright Ordinance.
223. Section 60(2) of the Copyright Ordinance.
224. Section 60(3) of the Copyright Ordinance.

program if the copying or adapting is necessary for his or her lawful use.[225] It specifically provides the possibility of copying or adapting the program for the purpose of correcting errors.[226]

222. Section 64 of the ordinance enables computer programs and other works in electronic form to be transferred from the purchaser to a second purchaser and so on, subject to certain conditions. There is no problem when the software contract expressly includes a provision on transferring. If there are no express terms prohibiting the transfer of the copy by the purchaser: imposing obligations which continue after a transfer; prohibiting the assignment of any licence or terminating any licence on a transfer; or providing for the terms on which a transferee may do the things which the purchaser was permitted to do, anything which the purchaser was allowed to do may also be done without infringement of copyright by a transferee; but any copy, adaptation or copy of an adaptation made by the purchaser which is not also transferred is to be treated as an infringing copy for all purposes after the transfer.[227]

223. Regardless of the manner of licensing software, several important items are essential for most software contracts: scope of use (exclusivity, sublicensing), medium or technological environment for the use of the software; access restrictions; payment; the length of the agreement; amendment or alteration of the software; liability; technical protections; copyright notice and termination. To assist large-volume users of programs and avoid software piracy, many software developers offer site licences, under which the purchaser pays a fee to the manufacturer to make a specified number of copies of a particular program. In turn, the buyer agrees to keep an accurate record of who makes the copies and the computer or network on which they are installed.[228]

225. Section 61(1) of the Copyright Ordinance.
226. Section 61(2) of the Copyright Ordinance.
227. Section 64(2) of the Copyright Ordinance.
228. J.A. Senn, *Information Technology in Business: Principles, Practices and Opportunities* 673 (2d ed. Prentice Hall 1998).

Chapter 3. Turnkey Contracts

224. Turnkey is an IT industry term that refers to a complete system for a particular set of applications, such that the buyer needs to only turn the key to operate the system. Such systems normally involve custom application software and user-friendly interfaces so that the buyer's employees can operate the system with little or no training. Hong Kong is also developing its IT through such arrangements. Early in 1998, Nokia supplied full turnkey GSM 1,800 network expansion to New World Personal Communication Services, Hong Kong, which has been rather successful.[229] Some important turnkey projects have been conducted in Hong Kong, which generally include three primary areas: software development services, traffic engineering services and systems engineering services.[230]

225. The services provided a range from product concept to design, procurement and manufacture. In addition to the design and development of a software programme, which is the core component of our software development services, they also provide pre-solution consultancy and product planning and design prior to software development. A flexible approach to manufacturing shall be adopted to integrate with vendor-designated manufacturers and/or designers. The provider can order all parts, perform all assembly, test and audit to the stated standards, and pack and ship to a specified destination. Various warranty levels shall be available subject to manufacture terms and conditions. Most of the time production yield analysis provides valuable engineering feedback and ensures that the manufacturing process is constantly refined.

226. Software development services include the design and development of a suite of software programs to provide all the required functions together with a user-friendly man-machine interface. For example, a graphics-based, user-friendly man-machine interface was developed as part of the software services. Software services can also cover production of operation and maintenance manuals, operator training and software warranty services.

227. Traffic engineering services include the design and generation of traffic response plans to address normal, incident and emergency traffic plans, which includes the generation of an interlocking matrix to ensure safe operations and the identification of traffic parameters and their calibration for automatic incident detection.

---

229. Press Releases, Nokia Supplies Full Turnkey GSM 1800 Network Expansion to New World PCS, Hong Kong, 1 Jan. 1998 (available at https://www.globenewswire.com/NewsRoom?page=248335).
230. For example, Lantau Fixed Crossing-Traffic Control and Surveillance System; Western Harbour Crossing-Traffic Control & Surveillance System.

228. System engineering services involve providing assistance in the procurement, testing and commissioning of all equipment and systems; preparing system proposals for the central computer system; and defining interface requirements with other sub-systems.

229. Website development agreements can be a typical turnkey example in e-commerce. The objectives of a website development agreement are to ensure that the customers receive the website they have requested and to agree on the developer's obligations to create the site within an agreed time frame. The contract can contain several matters: content and design; ownership of intellectual property rights; source code;[231] acceptance testing;[232] warranties; deadlines; payment mechanisms; customers' obligations; and security. As far as security is concerned, especially when the intended website is for financial purposes, the guideline entitled *Security of Banking Transactions* over the Internet[233] published by the Hong Kong Monetary Authority (HKMA) shall have some relevance. The HKMA suggests that failure to maintain adequate accounting systems and adequate systems of control to safeguard Internet banking services could result in the bank being in breach of its obligations under the Seventh Schedule to the Banking Ordinance's 'Minimum Criteria for Authorization'.[234] Further reference can be made to 'Guidelines for Registered Persons Using the Internet to Collect Applications for Securities in an Initial Public Offering' published by the Hong Kong Securities and Futures Commission.[235] From the descriptions above, we can see that the provider shall undertake all the services before transferring the project to the client. While providing the services, the developer and customer should be attentive to several relevant laws concerning specific activities. Furthermore, the provider needs to provide the necessary technological assistance even at a later stage. Thus, such contracts can be vital, especially in the case when necessary expertise or resources are missing. This can significantly shorten the period and minimize financial sources needed to develop a project.

231. The source code is necessary for reading or modifying the programme. The customer should require the website developer to provide it with an updated copy of the source code upon completion of the website.
232. The agreement shall provide the customer with the opportunity to test the website to ensure that it performs in accordance with its functional and performance requirements.
233. https://www.hkma.gov.hk/media/eng/doc/code_eng.pdf.
234. Banking Ordinance (Cap. 155), Seventh Sch., para. 10.
235. https://www.sfc.hk/-/media/EN/assets/components/codes/files-previous/web/guidelines/guidelines-for-electronic-public-offerings/Guidelines-for-Registered-Persons-using-the-Internet-to-Collect-Applications-for-Securities-in-an-IP.pdf.

Chapter 4. Distribution Agreements

230. Under the Import and Export (Registration) Regulations (Cap. 60E), any person who imports an article into Hong Kong other than an exempted article will be required to lodge an import declaration with the Custom and Excise Department within fourteen days of import.

231. The Import and Export (Strategic Commodities) Regulations (Cap. 60G) require that all persons importing or exporting strategic commodities first obtain a licence from the Trade and Industry Department. The procedure for obtaining a licence is generally quick and inexpensive.

232. The regulations are especially relevant to encryption products. Certain kinds of software and technology, particularly encryption products, will require an import licence.

233. After importing into Hong Kong, one of the best ways to sell products in Hong Kong has been the use of distributors, which can also minimize the initial investment in the market. There are, indeed, a wide range of companies in Hong Kong which serve as distributors or agents for foreign merchants. Distributors take orders in the supplier's name. Distributors act in their own name and may stock products purchased from the manufacturer for resale. The choice shall depend on the relationship with which the manufacturer/supplier is most comfortable and the nature of the business.[236]

234. There are several types of distributors in Hong Kong ranging from those who simply stock retail stores with standard items to those providing sales, engineering and technical support for complex systems. Thus, it is common for a single company to deal in a wide variety of products in a particular sector.[237]

235. The development of electronic software distribution is a major breakthrough in distribution management. It primarily focused on Local Area Networks (LANs) management and on distributing new applications and updates of client software over local networks and organizational enterprise networks.[238] The development has not been linear; instead, there are improvements in the system to cut costs and improve timelines, while using data to facilitate the delivery of services. Hong Kong does not have any special legislation on distribution. With the electronic distribution, reference can be made to laws on protection of intellectual property rights as discussed in Part II. Generally, both parties are free to put into their

---

236. *Country Commercial Guide for FY 1995–1996: Hong Kong*, US Department of State (available at https://www.trade.gov/hong-kong-country-commercial-guide).
237. *Ibid.*
238. M. Nemzow, *Building Cyberstores: Installation, Transaction Processing, and Management* 387 (McGraw-Hill 1997).

agreements anything they both agree on, including restrictions on territory and a grace period for termination of the agreement. The items to be included in the agreement include:

(a) discussion of exclusivity and sales territories;
(b) discussion of proprietary information (intellectual property rights, piracy, etc.);
(c) levels of sales activity: set specific targets and goals to qualify for maintaining or renewing the agreement;
(d) time duration;
(e) payment terms;
(f) quality control: inspection and verification;
(g) rules of law: the applicable law and the authority for resolving possible disputes;
(h) covenants restricting activity following cancellation of the contract.[239]

239. *Ibid.*

Chapter 5. Maintenance Contracts

236. No specific rules exist in Hong Kong in regulating maintenance services. However, general rules on contracts for the supply of services shall apply. Thus, relevant rules in the Supply of Services (Implied Terms) Ordinance (SSITO) (Cap. 457), the Unconscionable Contracts Ordinance (Cap. 458) shall be valid for application for maintenance contracts.

237. Maintenance contracts can provide maintenance professionals with the right information, at the right time, at the right place, to support sound, strategic and tactical decision making. In the ICT field, such contracts aim to keep the computer running with maximum efficiency, most problems and faults can be detected early before they become more serious problems in the future.

238. Generally speaking, the following services can be provided:

(a) diagnostic check of major hardware components;
(b) registry checking and repairing;
(c) troubleshooting and presenting concerns and problems;
(d) removing casing and cleaning interior of system;
(e) updating current antivirus software;
(f) running ScanDisk and Disk Defragmenter;
(g) removing unnecessary *.chk and temporary files;
(h) cleaning mouse and keyboard;
(i) cleaning monitor with anti-static solution;
(j) cleaning CD and floppy disk drives;
(k) analysis and recommendations on upgrades;
(l) advise on running regular system backups and how to restore files in an emergency.

239. Three types of maintenance contracts can be offered:

(a) *Full-Service Maintenance Contract*: covers all repairs and all labour on a twenty-four-hour basis. The customer pays one annual fee for this contract. Full maintenance contracts can be written utilizing the customer's insurance.
(b) *Inspection and Maintenance Contract*: covers routine maintenance and inspections and can be written to include some parts. Emergency service and repairs are generally provided at reduced rates.
(c) One-*Stop Inspection Contract*: used mainly for certain facilities that are shut down during winter months. Annual maintenance is performed during the shutdown period.[240] As stated in the Entech Service Contract, Entech currently has the versatility and expertise to write a contract to meet all service requirements. Contracts are written entirely using in-house staff to eliminate subcontractor mark-ups, inter-company coordination and incidents. And Entech can now do

240. Available at www.entechsales.com.

preventive maintenance, full maintenance and bespoke functions. Preventive maintenance typically means that the contract provides checks, calibrations and detailed reports to ensure the system is running efficiently, and full maintenance will provide the customer with fixed maintenance costs and quality service, including regular inspections, emergency service calls and replacement parts. Bespoke services are designed to meet the needs of customers who are looking for a 'labour only' contract or a contract that falls between preventative and comprehensive maintenance.

240. With technological development, it is now possible to offer remote monitoring of sites via dedicated phone lines, with PC-driven control of equipment. The service charge will generally depend on customer location, number of units and unit condition. While making specific reference to the ICT maintenance contract, one should not forget web hosting agreements, which deal with the ongoing hosting and maintenance of websites once they have been developed. Web hosting services are offered either by sharing facilities on an existing server or the lease of equipment maintained by the host or a co-location arrangement. Several items can be included in such agreements: protection of data; response time; access to performance information; content liability; termination, etc.

Chapter 6. Facilities Management

241. With the increasing use of the Internet as a means to carry out activities, the market for facilities management in this field has and will continue to become more fragmented as customers require suppliers to produce contracts tailored to their own individual needs. Facilities management can involve quite a lot of services, which can include installing a fully integrated and secure online system (hardware and software), system maintenance, training and marketing support.

242. Furthermore, the scope of service can include providing telecommunications surveys and contract negotiations/installation management, security system recommendations, design and installation management, etc. The broadening of services is still moving forward, areas of growth include consultancy, IT (like recycling of electrical equipment and waste management) and services relating to the business process (such as tax compliance or human resources).[241] Another trend is the standardization of such contracts, which can shorten the time for negotiation; however, this can also involve certain risks. The customers might need extra services in obtaining advice on the suitability of the suppliers and the contents of such contracts.

243. By using customized software, facilities can be managed to ensure that the equipment will never miss a regular service; maintenance tasks can be performed on time and essential repairs be carried out. Depending on the customers' needs, facilities management can be provided through mobile engineers or, for larger sites with daily maintenance requirements, resident personnel based at the customer's site can be provided and dedicated solely to the customer. There has been rapid growth in companies offering software and solutions in facilities management. For example, Post-COVID-19, IBM has promoted their FMS by proclaiming to: optimize space and facility utilization; deliver a better occupant experience; create more efficient reporting; streamline lease administration and accounting.

241. *The Forces Driving Facilities Management Contracts*, 3 Dec. 2001 (available at www.bsee.co.uk).

Chapter 7. Network Services

244. With the development of the Internet, new intermediaries have arisen. A typical one is the provision of network services. This can include a wide variety of services, like providing network connection, maintenance of networks, etc. For example, ISP agreements concern Internet access services. For regulation of such services, reference can be made to rules issued by the HKISPA. For example, An 'Anti-SPAM-Code of Practice' released by the HKISPA, the office of the Privacy Commissioner and OFTA as a joint initiative to guide ISPs to combat spam e-mails.[242] Furthermore, references can also be made to the Control of Exemption Clauses Ordinance (Cap. 71), the SSITO (Cap. 457) dealing with the validity of exemption clauses where one party to the contract is a consumer and implied terms in the ISP agreements respectively.

245. More specifically, four categories of network services can be differentiated:

(a) *Installation, Testing, Implementation and Training*: the equipment based on the project specifications shall be installed and configured according to the contract. Testing and troubleshooting can ensure the smooth functioning of the network at a later stage. Network management statistics shall be gathered to confirm functional integrity. A training programme can also be formulated for administrators to ensure the proper ongoing management and maintenance of the networks.
(b) *Network Connectivity*: the contract can offer every type of connectivity; such a contract will generally contain provisions concerning storage of data, response time, service levels and uptime requirements,[243] access to performance information, liability, termination.
(c) *IP Telephony*: services can be provided to support toll-quality voice, distributed and redundant architectures, ongoing service and support and a lower total cost of ownership model.
(d) *WLAN*: such networks are superior and cost-saving solutions to LAN access. Great benefits can be achieved with such services enhancing collaboration and productivity.

242. *Version 2.0*, 8 Jun. 2005 (available at www.hkispa.org.hk/antispam/cop.html).
243. The requirements are generally expressed as a percentage of availability of the website over a specified period.

Chapter 8. Government Contracts

246. In the areas of procurement and contracts, various levels of government have begun to use EDI and other e-commerce methods for Business-to-Government (B2G) transactions. By using e-commerce, governments can cut down costs and bring more efficient methods to the procurement process. Such practice has been adopted in negotiations, supply chain management, etc. A number of online companies have been partnering with government agencies in electronic payments for taxes, permits, utility bills and other transactions.[244] This practice is also in accordance with the goal of the government, which has put services on the websites.

247. The Government Supplies Department (now Government Logistics Department, GLD) is the central purchasing, storage and supply organization for the HKSAR Government, serving over eighty government departments and certain non-government organizations. Open tender is the normal practice for the GLD in making purchases.[245] The GLD does not have any preference for the course of goods or services from a specific country or organization. Decisions are made in compliance with tender specifications, competitiveness in price, back-up service and delivery. The government has established a bid challenge system to live up to its commitments under the WTO Agreement on Government Procurement.

248. Invitations to open tender are published in the *Gazette* of the HKSAR Government, some selected newspapers and also on the home page of the GLD.[246] The GLD also maintains a list of suppliers for sending the invitations. Those who want to be considered for inclusion in the list can apply to the Director of Government Supplies. The application should supply basic information about the organizations, the goods or services they offer, such as the Business Registration Certificate, company profile, annual report and product catalogues. The GLD shall be free to evaluate the information and decide whether to include it or not. Tenderers can have around six weeks to prepare the offers. Payments shall be made by check or telegraph transfer within thirty days upon acceptance of the goods. Government contracts are published monthly in the *Government Gazette* and on the Internet.[247]

249. Electronic transactions with the government shall satisfy several requirements identified in the Gazette Notice made under section 11(2) of the Electronic Transactions Ordinance (ETO) on format, manner and procedure for making an electronic submission to the government under law.

250. The Gazette Notice made under section 11(2) of the ETO sets out the rules to satisfy the required communications:

---

244. G.R. Simpson, *Putting Government on the Web*, 1 Wall St. J. B (17 May 2000).
245. The objective of the GLD to provide bureaux and departments of the HKSAR Government with professional, cost-effective and timely logistical support services in the areas of procurement and supplies, transport operation and management, as well as printing services, to enable them to serve the people of Hong Kong better. *See* further www.gld.gov.hk/.
246. *See* further www.gld.gov.hk/.
247. *See* generally www.gld.gov.hk/.

(a) electronic records in English shall be encoded in American Standard Code for Information Interchange (ASCII);
(b) electronic records in Chinese shall be encoded in Big-5 or ISO10646 standard;
(c) manner of sending electronic records can be through e-mail in the form of a disk or CD-ROM in ISO 9660 format;
(d) the file format for electronic records shall be Text File (TXT), Microsoft Rich Text Format(RTF), Hypertext Markup Language (HTML) format or Adobe Portable Document Format (Acrobat version);
(e) graphic file formats for electronic records shall be Encapsulated PostScript Files (EPSF), Tag Image File Format (TIFF), Windows BitMaps (BMP), Graphics Interchange Format (GIF) or Joint Photographic Experts Group (JPEG);
(f) digital signatures shall be required for electronic records if an ordinance or a form specified by an ordinance so requires;
(g) digital signatures shall be attached to electronic records in accordance with the Secure Multipurpose Internet Mail Extension (S/MIME) and the Public Key Cryptography Standards (PKCS).

Part IV. Electronic Transactions

Chapter 1. Legal Status of Electronic Transactions

§1. Regulatory Framework for Electronic Transactions

251. To promote the development of e-commerce in Hong Kong, the Legislative Council has been proposing a clear legal framework to enhance certainty and security in the conduct of electronic transactions since early 1999.

252. Four key principles have been formulated to guide the establishment of the legal framework:

(1) the framework should remove any legal impediments to the conduct of electronic transactions;
(2) the framework should provide certainty and security in the conduct of electronic transactions, thereby enhancing the confidence and trust of the public in carrying out such transactions;
(3) the framework should adopt a technology-neutral approach to cope with rapid technological changes; and
(4) the framework should adopt a minimalist regulatory approach so as not to unnecessarily constrain the development of e-commerce in the private sector.[248]

253. On 7 January 2000, the ETO (Cap. 553) was enacted with the aims to: give electronic records and digital signatures used in electronic transactions the same legal status as that of their paper-based counterparts; and establish a framework to promote and facilitate the operation of certificate authorities so as to ensure trust and security in electronic transactions. It establishes the legislative framework for the conduct of electronic transactions. The Electronic Transactions (Amendment) Ordinance 2004 was enacted and came into operation on 30 June 2004 to update and improve the ordinance. The improvements include: (a) giving legal recognition to other forms of electronic signature, in addition to digital signature, for transactions not involving the Government; (b) accepting the service of documents in the form of electronic record as satisfying the requirement of service by post or in person

248. LC Paper No. CB(1)709/98-99(01), *Legislative Council Panel on Information Technology and Broadcasting: Legal Framework for Electronic Transactions*, 11 Jan. 1999 (available at www-.legco.gov.hk).

under the statutory provisions set out in the proposed new Schedule 3 to the ETO; and (c) introducing changes relating to the assessment of CA so as to improve the operation of the voluntary recognition scheme for CAs with the aim to increase public confidence in electronic transactions.

254. Besides this new ordinance, we should also take notice of several relevant ordinances which remain applicable to electronic contracts. These ordinances include the Sale of Goods Ordinance (SGO) (Cap. 26), the SSITO (Cap. 457), and the Control of Exemption Clauses Ordinance (Cap. 71).

§2. Application Scope of the ETO

255. The ETO covers the following:

(a) providing legal recognition to electronic records and digital signatures in electronic transactions (essentially making it clear that transactions conducted using paper documents and transactions conducted using electronic communications should be treated equally by the law); and
(b) establishing the framework necessary to promote and facilitate the operation of CAs.

256. However, certain exemptions in Electronic Transactions (Exclusion) Order subsequent to section 11(1) of the ETO have been provided, which include:

(a) certain generic items such as wills, trusts, statutory declarations, affidavits, powers of attorney, court orders, warrants, bills of exchange, documents or instruments concerning land or property transactions, etc., are exempted from the operation of the relevant provisions of the ETO;
(b) a mechanism is provided to exempt, by means of subsidiary legislation, specific rules of law from the operation of the relevant provisions in the ETO;[249]
(c) judicial proceedings are exempt from the operation of the relevant provisions in the ETO and the Court Rules Committees are empowered to apply the relevant provisions to such proceedings when the relevant courts/tribunals are ready;[250] and
(d) a mechanism is provided for format and procedural requirements to be specified if necessary in respect of cases whereby electronic information is accepted under a rule of law.

249. For example, ss 5–8 of the Electronic Transactions Ordinance shall not apply to the Hong Kong Special Administrative Region Passports Appeal Board established under the Hong Kong Special Administrative Region Passports (Appeal Board) Regulation (Cap. 539A sub. Leg.).
250. *See* further information in Court Proceedings (Electronic) Ordinance.

§3. The Requirement of 'Writing'

257. The ETO has clearly endowed electronic records with the same legal recognition as their paper-based counterparts. Section 2 of the ordinance defines the term 'electronic record' broadly to include records generated in digital form by an information system which can be transmitted within an information system or from one information system to another and stored in an information system or other media.

258. Section 2 further defines 'information system' as a system which automatically processes or records information in that system or in another system or can be used to process or retrieve information so stored or processed.

259. On the question of whether electronic contracts can be considered as a 'writing', the ordinance provides that:

(1) if a rule of law requires or permits information to be given or presented in writing, the use of electronic records will satisfy that rule of law; however, the information contained in the electronic record should be accessible so as to be usable for subsequent reference;[251]
(2) if a rule of law requires information to be retained, or to be presented or retained in the original form, that requirement is met by retaining or presenting the information in the form of electronic records; the conditions for the satisfaction are:
  (a) there exists a reliable assurance as to the integrity of the information from the time when it was first generated in its final form; and
  (b) where it is required that information be presented, the information is capable of being displayed in legible form to the person to whom it is to be presented.[252]
(3) contracts shall not be denied legal effect solely on the ground that electronic records are used in their formation, and electronic records shall not be denied admissibility as evidence in court on the sole ground that they are electronic records.[253]

260. Similar definitions can also be found in the Interpretation and General Clauses Ordinance (Cap. 1). 'Writing and printing' includes writing, printing, lithography, photography, typewriting and any other mode of representing words in a visible form.[254] Though the display on a screen is not permanent, such record is capable of subsisting in a visible form and should, therefore, be able to satisfy the legal definition of 'writing' in the present ordinance. Accordingly, an electronic contract shall not be denied its validity during implementation.

251. Section 5 of the Electronic Transactions Ordinance.
252. Section 7(1) of the Electronic Transactions Ordinance.
253. Section 9 of the Electronic Transactions Ordinance.
254. Section 3 of the Interpretation and General Clauses Ordinance.

261. For the validity of retention of information in electronic records, several requirements need to be satisfied (whether retained in writing or otherwise):

(a) the information contained in the electronic record remains accessible so as to be usable for subsequent reference;
(b) the relevant electronic record is retained in the format in which it was originally generated, sent or received, or in the format which can be demonstrated to represent accurately the information originally generated, sent or received; and
(c) the information which enables the identification of the origin and destination of the electronic record and the date and time when it was sent or received, is retained.[255]

§4. Formation of an Electronic Contract

262. The elements required for the formation of a contract have long been settled under the common law system: an offer, an acceptance, an intention to be legally bound[256] and consideration.[257] The basic elements regarding the formation of an electronic contract continue to be the same as those of a traditional contract.

263. An offer is a definite statement or conduct manifesting a willingness to enter into a contract. A statement may be an invitation to treat even though it contains the word 'offer'.[258] Acceptance requires that an offeree communicate his or her assent to the terms of the offer. Acceptance may be manifested by acts such as speaking or sending a letter, a telegram or other explicit or implicit communication to the offeror.[259]

264. There are two basic rules in defining the time of the formation of the contract: Receipt Rule and Mailbox Rule. According to the Receipt Rule, the acceptance must be received by the offeror before a contract can be formed. Under the traditional Mailbox Rule, an offeree's acceptance was effective when the offeree dispatched a letter out of his or her control. Delivery of an offer occurs when it is placed in the mailbox.[260] That is, once the acceptance leaves the hands of the offeree, the contract is considered formed.

265. Nevertheless, with e-mail and fax, the gap between dispatch and receipt is so small that the Mailbox Rule and the Receipt Rule are no longer a significant issue. No detailed guidance is provided by Hong Kong law as to which rule shall be applied. In instantaneous communication, an e-mail which bounces back cannot be said to have been accepted. However once the message goes into the inbox, it has

255. Section 8(1) of the Electronic Transactions Ordinance.
256. *Rose and Frank Co. v. Crompton Bros Ltd.* [1923] 2 KB 261.
257. *Thomas v. Thomas* FL & K 621.
258. *Spencer v. Harding* (1870) LR 5 CP 561.
259. D.K. Srivastava ed., *Business Law in Hong Kong* 98–108 (2d ed. Sweet & Maxwell 2007).
260. *Adams v. Lindsell* (1818) 1 B & Ald 681.

been accepted even if it is unopened or unread. However, it should be noted that where the offeror has not designated an information system which will be used to enter into the contract, the electronic record must come to his or her knowledge, but this begs the question of what constitutes knowledge and whether constructive knowledge is sufficient. Suppose the offeror sees the message but chooses to ignore it because he or she wants to keep his or her options open, it is submitted that once the offeror becomes aware that the sender is trying to communicate with him or her, he or she ought to be treated as having knowledge of the sender's acceptance.[261]

266. Section 17 of the ordinance provides that an offer and acceptance may be expressed in whole or in part by electronic records unless the parties agree otherwise. A contract making use of an electronic record should not be denied its validity or enforceability on the sole ground that an electronic record was used for that purpose.[262]

267. Section 18, amended by Editorial No. 3 of 2017, offers rules on attribution, issuance and receipt of an electronic record. It states that in the absence of an agreement, the electronic record between the originator and the addressee of an electronic record is attributed to the originator, if it was sent by the originator, sent with the authority of the originator or sent by an information system programmed by or on behalf of the originator to operate and to send the electronic record automatically; the above provision shall not affect the laws on agency or the law on the formation of contract.[263]

268. While no rules are provided concerning the application of the Mailbox Rule or the Receipt Rule, the ordinance does offer the rules as to the time when an electronic record is deemed sent and received. Section 19 specifies the time of sending and receiving electronic records. Unless the originator and the addressee of an electronic record otherwise agree, an electronic record is deemed to have been sent when it is accepted by an information system outside the control of the originator or of the person who sent the electronic record on behalf of the originator. Furthermore, if not agreed otherwise by the originator and the addressee of an electronic record, the time of receipt is deemed to be made when the electronic record is accepted by the designated information system if the addressee has designated an information system for the purpose of receiving electronic records.

269. If the electronic record is sent to an information system of the addressee that is not the designated information system, or if the addressee has no designated information system, receipt is deemed to be made at the time the electronic record comes to the knowledge of the addressee. In this section, the term 'originator' means a person, by whom, or on whose behalf, the electronic record is sent or generated. The term 'addressee' refers to a person who is specified by the originator to

261. *See* further P. Stephenson, et al., *Cyberlaw in Hong Kong* 392–394 (2d ed. LexisNexis 2007).
262. Section 17 (1)–(2) of the Electronic Transactions Ordinance.
263. Section 18 of the Electronic Transactions Ordinance.

receive the electronic record. 'Intermediary' is a person who, on behalf of a person, sends, receives or stores that electronic record or provides other incidental services in respect of that electronic record.

270. The ordinance further provides rules on the place of business: a record will be regarded as having been sent from the place of business of the originator and received at the place of business of the addressee, even though the information system is not located at the place of the business.[264] In case there is more than one place of business, the principal place of business shall be that:

(a) which has the closest relationship to the underlying transaction; or
(b) if there is no underlying transaction, the principal place of business of the originator or the addressee; or
(c) if either party does not have a place of business, the place where the originator or addressee ordinarily resides.[265]

§5. Implied Terms: The SGO and the SSITO

271. The terms of a contract can be express terms and implied terms. Express terms are clearly incorporated into the contract, clearly showing the intention of both parties to be bound by the contract.[266] Implied terms are not clearly written in the contract. Such terms can exist for business efficacy[267] or from deduction of a course of previous dealings.[268] Nevertheless, several ordinances also provide certain implied terms in some contracts.

272. The SGO applies to goods sold by a merchant to a buyer in Hong Kong. The provision that has the closest relation to the present discussion has been the rule for implied terms. While some terms have been clearly provided in electronic contracts, the SGO defines implied terms in the contract for sales, which include warranties, risk of loss, payment and delivery terms. The warranties include fitness for a particular purpose, merchantability, title, conformance to description and conformance to sample.[269] However, it is to be noted that the SGO probably does not apply to software sold electronically by clickwrap.[270]

273. The SSITO (Cap. 457) provides implied terms in services contracts; however, such terms can be expressly excluded by the parties. For example, under the

264. Section 19(4) of the Electronic Transactions Ordinance.
265. Section 19(5) of the Electronic Transactions Ordinance.
266. *Olley v. Marlborough Court Ltd.* [1949] 1 KB 532.
267. *Shirlaw v. Southern Foundries (1926) Ltd.* [1939] 2 KB 206.
268. *Hardwick Game Farm v. Suffolk Agricultural and Poultry Producers' Association Ltd.* [1966] 1 ALL ER 309.
269. *See* further ss 13–16 of the SGO (Cap. 26).
270. P. Tan, *E-com Legal Guide: Hong Kong* (Baker & McKenzie January 2001).

SSITO the supplier must warrant that the services will be performed with reasonable care and diligence;[271] and if commercial terms are not specified, the services will be performed within a reasonable time and for a reasonable price.[272]

§6. The Control of Exemption Clauses Ordinance

274. This ordinance is not specifically directed at electronic transactions; however, some provisions can be quoted in certain situations, in particular when liability is concerned. The ordinance puts some restrictions on exemption clauses which concern:

(a) death or personal injury resulting from negligence;[273]
(b) loss or damage arising from defective consumer goods in the course of usage or resulting from the negligence in the course of manufacture or distribution of goods;[274]
(c) contractual duty relating to quality of goods, but it only applies if the injured party is a consumer;[275]
(d) contractual duty relating to transfer of title or possession of goods sold or supplied.[276]

275. Reasonableness is also a very important element in deciding the validity of the exemption clause. The party who seeks to rely on the exemption clause should prove that the clause is in accordance with rule of law and it is fair to rely on the clause.[277] Furthermore, several factors shall be applied in testing reasonableness: the language used; the resources available to the person invoking the clause for the purpose of meeting the liability, should it arise.[278]

§7. Bills Committee on Import and Export (Electronic Transactions) Bill 2001

276. Various ordinances have been amended for the use of electronic means in carrying out certain transactions.[279] The affected ordinances include: the Import and Export Ordinance (Cap. 60); the Reserved Commodities Ordinance (Cap. 296); the

271. Section 5 of the SSITO.
272. Sections 6(1) and 7(1) of the SSITO.
273. Section 7 of the Control of Exemption Clauses Ordinance.
274. Section 10 of the Control of Exemption Clauses Ordinance.
275. Section 11(2), (3) of the Control Exemption Clauses Ordinance.
276. Section 11(1), (4) of the Control Exemption Clauses Ordinance.
277. *St Albans City and District Council v. International Computers Ltd.* [1996] 4 ALL ER 481.
278. Section 3 of the Control of Exemption Clauses Ordinance.
279. To enact an Ordinance, the Law Drafting Division of the Department of Justice of Hong Kong shall set up a drafting committee, the draft is termed as 'bill'. For further information on this specific committee, *see* legco.gov.hk/yr01-02/english/bills/brief/b46_brf.pdf.

Industrial Training (Clothing Industry) Ordinance (Cap. 318); and the Protection of Non-Government Certificates of Origin Ordinance (Cap. 324).

§8. Jurisdiction and Choice of Law

277. Jurisdiction is the power of a court to hear and decide a case. Choice of jurisdiction is an important issue for e-commerce since parties are often from different jurisdictions whose laws differ from each other substantially. So far, Hong Kong has not acceded to any international conventions or agreements on jurisdiction. The courts of Hong Kong will, first of all, give effect to an express choice of jurisdiction in a contract. When there is no express choice of jurisdiction, the courts will look to whether the defendants reside in Hong Kong. If no defendants reside in Hong Kong, the courts will look to other general factors such as whether Hong Kong is the most appropriate and convenient forum. For example, the fact that the contract was essentially made and performed in Hong Kong, although all parties are overseas, would also be a persuasive factor.[280] The aim of the court is to identify the forum in which the case can be suitably tried in the interest of justice and in the interest of all the involved parties.[281] No special rules exist relating to consumer contracts. Accordingly, consumer contracts entered into in Hong Kong will be dealt with in the same way as any other contracts. Nevertheless, special rules of other states should be taken into account.

278. Once the issue of jurisdiction is settled, the court must determine the applicable law to decide the case. The express choice of law of the parties to the contract shall be respected by the courts of Hong Kong, as long as their choice is in good faith, is legal and is not contrary to public policy.[282] Where no choice of law is expressly made, the courts will look at several factors to find the implied choice of the parties. The factors can include previous dealings; choice of jurisdiction; reference to a legal system; use of a language or reference to particular legal terminology and currency.[283]

279. When there is no choice as stated above, the courts shall apply the general private international law rules to decide the applicable law. The courts will generally look for the law with which the facts of the case have the most real and substantial connection.[284] Several factors shall be taken into account when deciding on such connections: the place where the contract was entered into; where performance will occur; the location and nature of the subject matter of the contract; and the domicile of the parties to the contract.

---

280. *The Abidin Daver* [1984] AC 398; [1984] 1 ALL ER 470, HL.
281. *Spilada Maritime Corp. v. Cansulex Ltd., The Spilada* [1987] AC 460, at 480; [1986] 3 ALL ER 843 at 858, HL, per Lord Goff.
282. *Vita Food Products Inc. v. Unus Shipping Co. Ltd.* [1939] AC 277.
283. *See* further C. Wright, W. McAuliffe & A. Gamvros, *Internet Law in Hong Kong* 381 (Sweet & Maxwell 2003).
284. *Amin Rasheed Shipping Corp. v. Kuwait Insurance Co., The Al Wahab* [1984] AC 50; [1983] 2 ALL ER 884, HL.

280. While the parties are free to choose any applicable law to the contract, they will be subject to certain rules relating to consumer contracts. These rules include the Unconscionable Contracts Ordinance (Cap. 458) and the Control of Exemption Clauses Ordinance (Cap. 71).

Chapter 2. Regulation of Electronic Signatures and Certification Services

§1. Background

281. The HKSAR Government has adopted a three-pronged approach in establishing a digital signature framework to drive e-commerce under the 'Digital 21' IT Strategy.[285] The first prong is to build a digital signature infrastructure for the conduct of secure electronic transactions. The second is the establishment of a public CA, and the third is for the government to adopt PKI technology in the delivery of public services.[286]

282. In some cases, physical signatures are not a necessary element in giving validity to a document in Hong Kong. In case of a missing signature, the party seeking to enforce the contract shall be obliged to show that the other party was aware or should have been aware of its terms and agreed to them. Transactions involving land, deeds (which must be executed under seal) and assignment of copyright require signatures. Signatures are the main method of evidencing the fact that an agreement has been reached.

283. To provide legal recognition to electronic records and digital signatures, the Legislative Council has further proposed that the United Nations Commission on International Trade Law (UNCITRAL) – Model Law on Electronic Commerce shall be the model for the present purpose in Hong Kong. Some stipulations are laid out as follows:

(a) information shall not be denied legal effect solely on the ground that it is in the form of electronic records;
(b) where the law requires information to be provided in writing, that requirement is met by electronic records;
(c) where the law requires information to be presented or retained, that requirement is met by presenting or retaining the information in the form of electronic records;
(d) electronic records shall not be denied admissibility as evidence in court solely because they are in the form of electronic records;
(e) messages shall not be denied legal effect in the formation of contracts solely on the ground that they are in the form of electronic records; and
(f) where the law requires a signature of a person, that requirement is met by a digital signature which shall have the same effect as a hand-written signature.[287]

---

285. *See* further *2001 Hong Kong Digital 21 Strategy: Connecting the World* (available at https://www.ogcio.gov.hk/en/news/publications/doc/2001_digital21.pdf).
286. Digital Signature Framework to Boost E-commerce, 30 Sep. 2000, at www.chinadaily.com.cn.
287. The Law Society of Hong Kong's Submissions on the Electronic Transactions Bill, 9 Nov. 1999, LC Paper No. CB (1) 343/99-00(03) (available at www.legco.gov.hk/yr98-99/english/bc/bc19/papers/343e03.pdf).

§2. Electronic Signature and Digital Signature

284. 'Signature' is a rather broad term, which can include any symbol executed or adopted, or any methodology or procedure employed or adopted, by a person with the intention of authenticating or approving a record.[288] Generally speaking, typing your name at the end of an e-mail shall suffice as a valid signature; however, there could be arguments on the forms of automatic attachment, the truth of the signature, etc. Electronic signature could provide the ideal solution which makes use of an electronic representation of a person's name.

285. The general trend is that an electronic signature shall be accorded the same validity as the traditional signature. 'Electronic signature' is defined as any letters, characters, numbers or other symbols in digital form attached to or logically associated with an electronic record and executed or adopted for the purpose of authenticating or approving the electronic record.[289]

286. If a rule of law requires the signature of a person (the first-mentioned person) on a document or provides for certain consequences if a document is not signed by the first-mentioned person and neither the first-mentioned person nor the person to whom the signature is to be given (the second-mentioned person) is or is acting on behalf of a government entity, an electronic signature of the first-mentioned person satisfies the requirement if:

(a) the first-mentioned person uses a method to attach the electronic signature to or logically associate the electronic signature with an electronic record for the purpose of identifying himself or herself and indicating his or her authentication or approval of the information contained in the document in the form of the electronic record;
(b) having regard to all the relevant circumstances, the method used is reliable, and is appropriate, for the purpose for which the information contained in the document is communicated; and
(c) the second-mentioned person consents to the use of the method by the first-mentioned person.[290]

287. Before around 2003, digital signature was the only technically mature technology that provided security service of a quality that satisfied the need for user authentication, ensuring the integrity and confidentiality of data and protecting non-repudiation of transactions.[291] A digital signature satisfies the requirement if it is supported by a recognized certificate; generated within the validity of that certificate; and used in accordance with the terms of that certificate.[292]

288. Section 2 of the Electronic Transactions Ordinance.
289. *Ibid.*
290. Section 6(2) of the Electronic Transactions Ordinance.
291. *See* the Hong Kong Government's Response to Comments made by the Hong Kong Computer Society, LC Paper No. CB (1)297/99-00(04).
292. Section 6(1)(A) of the Electronic Transactions Ordinance.

288. 'Digital signature', in relation to an electronic record, means an electronic signature of the signer generated by the transformation of the electronic record using an asymmetric cryptosystem and a hash function such that a person having the initial untransformed electronic record and the signer's public key can determine:

(a) whether the transformation was generated using the private key that corresponds to the signer's public key; and
(b) whether the initial electronic record has been altered since the transformation was generated.[293]

289. From the broad interpretation, typing the name at the end could suffice so long as the court is satisfied that the signer had the required intention to authenticate at the time of signature.

290. To clarify the term 'within the validity of that certificate', the ordinance continues to define as at the time the digital signature is generated:

(a) the recognition of the recognized certificate is not revoked or suspended;
(b) if the Director of IT Services has specified a period of validity for the recognition of the recognized certificate, the certificate is within that period; and
(c) if the recognized CA has specified a period of validity for the recognized certificate, the certificate is within that period.[294]

291. It should be noted that the ordinance provides several exceptions to the general rules (i.e., sections 5–8 which deal with electronic records and digital signatures shall not be applicable to the following situations) which include:

(a) requirement or permission for information to be given in writing;
(b) requirement for the signature of a person;
(c) requirement for information to be presented or retained in its original form;
(d) requirement for information to be retained;
(e) gazetted orders with opposite requirement;
(f) special requirements for the manner and format of electronic records;
(g) special requirements for court and tribunal proceedings;
(h) specific provisions as to electronic records in other ordinances;
(i) consent between private parties;
(j) other statutory requirements.[295]

---

293. Section 2 of the Electronic Transactions Ordinance.
294. Section 6(1) of the Electronic Transactions Ordinance.
295. For further provisions, *see* s. 3 and Part IV of the Electronic Transactions Ordinance.

§3. PUBLIC KEY INFRASTRUCTURE

292. An asymmetric cryptosystem has been adopted for digital signatures. This, in contrast to a symmetric cryptosystem, which involves a single key known to the sender and recipient of the message and the same key, is used to encrypt and decrypt the message by the sender and recipient respectively. The latter system entails a danger during transmission of the key. Thus, the asymmetric cryptosystem is safer; as defined by the ordinance, it means a system capable of generating a secure key pair, consisting of a private key for generating a digital signature and a public key to verify the digital signature.[296]

§4. CERTIFICATION SERVICES

293. A CA is a third-party entity whose business it is to issue and revoke certificates that establish the validity of public keys. This entity is the trusted third party that vouches for the user's identity and issues public key certificates.[297] The HKSAR Government has agreed to take the lead in the development of a PKI in Hong Kong. To protect consumer interests and increase consumers' confidence in electronic transactions, government recognition shall be granted only to CAs:

(a) which have achieved a trust standard acceptable to the government; and
(b) which adopt common and open standards in their operation, thus ensuring interoperability with other recognized CAs under the local PKI.

294. Furthermore, for CAs to obtain recognition, several requirements should be satisfied:

(a) the publication of a certification practice statement which clearly specifies the practices employed in issuing digital certificates to subscribers;
(b) the use of a trustworthy system in performing CA services;
(c) the engagement of an accredited computer security professional to conduct an annual audit on the provision of CA services; and
(d) the compliance with a code of practice issued by the government.[298]

295. In determining whether an application is suitable for recognition as a CA, the Director of the IT Services shall take into account the following:

(a) whether the applicant has the appropriate financial status for operating as a recognized CA in accordance with this ordinance and the code of practice;
(b) the arrangements put in place or proposed to be put in place by the applicant to cover any liability that may arise from his or her activities relevant for the purposes of this ordinance;

296. Section 2 of the Electronic Transactions Ordinance.
297. M. Rustad & C. Daftary, *E-Business Legal Handbook*, 135, Aspen L. & Bus. (2001).
298. Section 20(3) of the Electronic Transactions Ordinance.

(c) the system, procedure, security arrangements and standards used or proposed to be used by the applicant to issue certificates to subscribers;
(d) any report or statutory declaration furnished by the applicant under section 20(3);
(e) whether the applicant and the responsible officers are fit and proper persons; and
(f) the reliance limits set or proposed to be set by the applicant for his or her certificates.[299]

296. The ETO further defines the factors to be considered in understanding the term 'a fit and proper person':

(a) the fact that the person has a conviction in Hong Kong or elsewhere for an offence for which it was necessary to find that the person had acted fraudulently, corruptly or dishonestly;
(b) the fact that the person has been convicted of an offence against this ordinance;
(c) if the person is an individual, the fact that the person is an undischarged bankruptcy debtor or has entered into a composition or a scheme of arrangement or a voluntary arrangement within the meaning of the Bankruptcy Ordinance (Cap. 6) within five years preceding the date of the application; and
(d) if the person is a body corporate, the fact that the person is in liquidation, is the subject of a winding-up order or there is a receiver appointed in relation to it or it has entered into a composition or a scheme of arrangement or a voluntary arrangement within the meaning of the Bankruptcy Ordinance (Cap. 6) within five years preceding the date of the application.[300]

297. The Director of the IT Services may recognize certificates issued by a recognized CA as recognized certificates upon application by that authority.[301] However, under certain circumstances, the director can also revoke or suspend recognition.[302]

298. To decide upon whether to revoke or suspend, besides the factors having been considered during the determination of awarding the certificate, the director needs to consider several other factors:

(a) whether the CA has failed:
  (i) to operate in accordance with the certification practice statement;
  (ii) to comply with the code of practice;
  (iii) to use a trustworthy system; or
  (iv) to comply with any provision of this ordinance; and

299. Section 21(4) of the Electronic Transactions Ordinance.
300. Section 21(5) of the Electronic Transactions Ordinance.
301. Section 22(1) of the Electronic Transactions Ordinance.
302. Sections 23, 24 of the Electronic Transactions Ordinance.

(b) any report statutory declaration furnished by the CA under section 43(1) or 43A(1).[303]

299. In connection with this, the government has invited the Hong Kong Post to serve as the public CA by the end of 1999 on a non-exclusive basis and to establish the necessary PKI. This can be seen as an attempt by the Hong Kong Government to take the initiative in the establishment of a recognized CA in Hong Kong as the business of CA is novel to Hong Kong and it is uncertain whether the Hong Kong businessmen have interest in this new business.[304]

300. The Hong Kong Post launched the world's first mobile e-Cert system in October 2001. As provided in the ETO, the Postmaster General is a recognized CA for the purposes of this ordinance.[305] The new mobile e-Certs will be available for individuals and businesses to authenticate their identities over various types of mobile devices, including PDAs and mobile handsets. A company or other bodies in the business of issuing certificates within the definition of the ordinance can apply to the director to be recognized as a CA; such an application is entirely voluntary.

301. A certificate means a record which:

(a) is issued by a CA for the purpose of supporting a digital signature which purports to confirm the identity or other significant characteristics of the person who holds a particular key pair;
(b) identifies the CA issuing it;
(c) names or identifies the person to whom it is issued;
(d) contains the public key of the person to whom it is issued; and
(e) is signed by a responsible officer of the CA issuing it.[306]

302. Again, the so-called recognized certificate means a valid certificate issued by a recognized CA that has been approved by the Director of IT Services.[307] A certificate usually contains: a subject name; a subject public key; an issuer name; notice of the validity period for the information;[308] a serial number; and an issuer's signature.[309] By issuing a recognized certificate, a recognized CA represents to any person who reasonably relies on the information contained in the certificate or a digital signature verifiable by the public key listed in the certificate that the recognized CA

303. Section 25 of the Electronic Transactions Ordinance.
304. R. Wu, *Electronic Transactions Ordinance-Building a Legal Framework for E-commerce in Hong Kong*, 1 J. Info., L. & Tech. (2000) (available at www2.warwick.ac.uk/fac/soc/law/elj/jilt/2000_1/wu).
305. Section 34 of the Electronic Transactions Ordinance.
306. Section 2 of the Electronic Transactions Ordinance.
307. *See* further s. 2 of the Electronic Transactions Ordinance.
308. *See* further s. 41(1) of the Electronic Transactions Ordinance: a recognized certification authority may specify a reliance limit in the certificate in issuing a recognized certificate.
309. M.S. Baum, *Secure Electronic Commerce, Doing Business and Avoiding Liability in Cyberspace* (Suffolk University Law School 10 May 1996).

has issued the certificate in accordance with any applicable certification practice statement incorporated by reference in the certificate or of which the relying person has noticed.[310]

303. Later, Tradelink joined as the second-recognized public CA for e-commerce. A digital signature will only be recognized as legally effective if it is supported by a certificate issued by a recognized CA and is generated during the validity of the certificate. If the CA is not recognized, the party alleging the validity of the contract will have the burden of proving his or her assertion, relying on the usual common law rules on contract. Thus, use of a non-complying digital signature might still support the existence of a contract, as long as it satisfies the common law requirements.

304. The Hong Kong Post will provide CA services to both the public and private sectors. Digi-Sign Certification Services Limited is a commercially recognized CA, which issues digital certificates under the brand name of 'ID-Cert' for both individuals and organisations. The ID-Certs can be used in a range of services such as Government e-services, online banking, online trading and other services involving the exchange of electronic documents. Any other authority has to apply to the Director of IT Services to become a recognized CA. The private sectors are welcome to set up CAs to serve the specific needs of individual sectors. There will be no exclusivity in CA operations. Thus the government recognized the need to examine the question of cross-referencing and mutual recognition of digital signatures among CAs so as to ensure that overall PKI will function effectively across different business sectors.

305. A recognized CA is generally not liable for any loss caused by reliance on a false or forged digital signature of a subscriber supported by a recognized certificate issued by that CA if the recognized CA has complied with the requirements of the ETO and the code of practice with respect to that certificate. It will also not be liable in excess of the amount specified in the certificate as its reliance limit, for a loss caused by reliance on any information:

(a) that the recognized CA is required to confirm according to the certification practice statement and the code of practice; and
(b) which is misrepresented on that recognized certificate or in a repository.[311]

§5. Subscriber Agreement for e-Cert

306. Since the Post has been designated as the CA, it formulates a model agreement for subscribers. As defined in the agreement, the Postmaster General is the recognized CA and acts as one party in the agreement. It is represented by the Hong Kong Post Office (HKPost).

310. Section 39 of the Electronic Transactions Ordinance.
311. Section 42 of the Electronic Transactions Ordinance.

307. Subscribers can be individuals, legal bodies and other entities. Separate contracts are offered for different bodies. Different types of certificates can be issued: e-Cert (Personal) Certificate; e-Cert (Organizational) Certificate; e-Cert (Server) Certificate and e-Cert (Encipherment) Certificate. Hong Kong Post CA has started issuing a new type of recognized digital certificates, namely iAM Smart-Certs, which are designated for the subscribers who are holders of 'iAM Smart+' account to conduct digital signing with legal backing under the ETO. With the prevalence of iAM Smart, this development is in line with e-governance initiative.

308. When reaching the agreement, the certification practice statement is automatically recognized and incorporated. By accepting the terms of the agreement, the subscriber shall be deemed to acknowledge an awareness of the operation of a PKI system; an understanding of the limits of such a system and an understanding of the necessity of maintaining the security of the private key related to the public key named in the digital certificate.[312] This agreement, including the incorporated statement, constitutes the entire agreement.

309. The agreement further defines the rights and obligations of both parties; according to procedures of issuing e-Cert, the HKPost undertakes limited liability in the services, which is also in accordance with the certification practice statement.

---

312. Article 5 of the Subscriber Agreement for E-Cert.

Chapter 3. Legal Aspects of Electronic Banking

§1. Background

310. Banking encompasses a broad range of financial services and products, some of which remain the province of real-world providers and others of which have been successfully migrated to the e-world. There are very few pure Internet banks: most operate closed systems with telephone support, and most are subsidiaries of or collaborations between established offline institutions.

311. In Hong Kong, the Internet has rapidly become a popular medium for provision of financial services. This can be best demonstrated by the development of e-banking. Smart cards are widely used to store and transfer funds electronically in Hong Kong.[313] The demand to use such services from a technologically aware population and the availability of the infrastructure functions as impetus to such a development. With financial institutions launching a myriad of Internet-based initiatives, Hong Kong may become a regional electronic financial centre. However, the regulatory framework in Hong Kong with respect to e-banking is still in its early stage of development.[314]

312. The Banking Ordinance is the primary legislation in Hong Kong to regulate banking activities. The HKMA acts as the sole regulator for banking activities in Hong Kong. It is established within the framework of the executive-led Hong Kong Government and is accountable to the Financial Secretary.

313. The objectives of the HKMA are the following:

- to maintain currency stability, within the framework of the linked exchange rate system, through sound management of the Exchange Fund, monetary policy operations and other means deemed necessary;
- to promote the safety and stability of the banking system through the regulation of banking business and the business of taking deposits, and the supervision of authorized institutions;
- to promote the efficiency, integrity and development of the financial system, particularly payment and settlement arrangements.

314. Bearing the objectives in mind, the HKMA performs the following functions:

313. These include: value access cards (such as typical credit and charge cards); stored value cards (such as Visa Cash and phone cards); and electronic purses (such as Mondex).

314. Internet Banking-Key Legal Considerations: Regional Overview-Hong Kong, Baker & McKenzie, Hong Kong, November 2000.

(a) formulation and implementation of monetary policy: to maintain exchange rate stability by implementing measures which improve the robustness of the monetary management system and conduct foreign exchange operations in accordance with the discipline of current board arrangements;
(b) exercising effective supervision of banking and deposit-taking institutions: to maintain the stability and integrity of the financial system, and to provide a measure of protection to depositors;
(c) managing the Exchange Fund with the objectives of preserving capital, ensuring that the entire monetary base will be at all times fully backed by highly liquid short-term US Dollar denominated securities, ensuring sufficient liquidity for the purpose of maintaining monetary and financial stability and achieving an investment return that will preserve the long-term purchasing power of the assets.[315]

315. It regulates the issuance of multipurpose stored value cards.[316] It can also, after consultation with the Financial Secretary, publish guidelines and circulars specifying business practices to be complied with by authorized institutions.[317] Since the Banking Ordinance does not contain any provision related to e-banking, the role of the guidelines appears more important.

316. The HKMA has released a number of guidelines on the subject. It supports the establishment of e-banks and e-banking services in Hong Kong. But it would have to ensure that this would not happen in a disruptive manner and any security system should be of a standard comparable to the current security standards applicable to conventional authorized institutions. A study group on e-banking was set up in July 1997 to enable the HKMA to keep abreast of developments in e-banking and assist in the development of appropriate policy and regulatory responses to technological developments.

§2. AUTHORIZATION OF E-BANKS

317. According to the Guidelines, authorized institutions[318] do not need to seek formal approval from the HKMA to offer their services through the Internet, but they should discuss their plans to do so with the HKMA in advance.

318. The matters to be discussed include the following:

---

315. Hong Kong Monetary Authority (available at www.info.gov.hk/hkma).
316. Banks licensed in Hong Kong have the authority to issue the multipurpose stored cards, though other types of businesses may apply to the HKMA for a licence to issue such cards. *See* HKMA, Ch. 10 Authorization of the Issue of Multi-Purpose Stored Value Cards, Guide to Authorisation, September 2002.
317. Section 82 of the Banking Ordinance.
318. The institutions refer to existing licensed banks which make use of the Internet or other electronic means as an alternative channel to deliver their products or services to customers.

(a) the business plan, including the timetable for the launch of the service, the types of products and services that would be included and the expected volume of transactions that would be conducted through the Internet;
(b) the contractual arrangements for liability arising from unauthorized or fraudulent transactions;
(c) the security arrangements for the system; in particular, what security measures have been/will be installed to:
   (i) restrict access to those users who are authorized to access the system;
   (ii) authenticate the identity and authority of the parties concerned to ensure the enforceability of transactions conducted through the Internet;
   (iii) maintain the secrecy of information while it is in passage over the communications network;
   (iv) ensure that the data has not been modified either accidentally or fraudulently while in passage on the communication network;
   (v) prevent unauthorized access to the institution's central computer system and database.
(d) the procedures and safeguards for monitoring unusual transactions and detection and investigation of possible fraud;
(e) any limit on the amount of transactions or any restrictions on the types of transfer that can be conducted through the Internet;
(f) whether the various security aspects of the system (including encryption/firewall/authentication techniques) have been reviewed by qualified independent consultants;
(g) what arrangements are in place to ensure that the risk management systems and internal controls are reviewed and evaluated on a regular basis (e.g., by external or internal auditors); and
(h) what the contingency plan is for major breaches in the security of the system including recovery procedures, damage control procedures and safeguarding the interests of customers.[319]

319. The HKMA further issued a guideline under section 16(10) of the Banking Ordinance concerning authorization of the so-called virtual bank. The guideline recognizes the applicability of the prudential criteria of conventional banks to the virtual bank. A physical presence shall be required for a virtual bank carrying on banking business in Hong Kong, but they need not establish physical branches.[320] The virtual bank should also have the necessary level of security for the business and construct appropriate policies, procedures and controls to deal with the particular risks to which it is exposed.[321] At a minimum, the applicant must go through eight basic types of risk identified in the risk-based supervisory framework of the MA (i.e., credit, interest rate, market, liquidity, operational, reputation, legal and

319. Guideline No. 15.1: Electronic Banking, HKMA, updated on 7 Jul. 1997 (available at http://www.hkma.gov.hk/eng/index.shtml).
320. Section 44 of the Banking Ordinance.
321. HKMA, Authorisation of Virtual Banks, A Guideline Issued by the MA under s. 16(10) of the Banking Ordinance, 5 May 2000.

strategic risk), analyse to what extent it will be subject to these risks as a virtual bank and establish appropriate controls to manage these risks.[322]

320. Furthermore, a virtual bank must be able to present a business plan which strikes an appropriate balance between the desire to build market share and the need to earn a reasonable return on assets and equity. The rights and obligations of the customers should be clearly stated in the terms and conditions for its service. The virtual banks may outsource their computer operations to a third-part y service provider, so long as it complies with HKMA's outsourcing guideline principles.

321. Locally incorporated virtual banks cannot be newly established other than through the conversion of an existing locally incorporated authorized institution. They should be at least 50% owned by a well-established bank or other supervised financial institution in good standing in the financial community with appropriate experience. If a locally incorporated virtual bank applicant is not owned by such a bank or financial institution, the HKMA expects the applicant to be held through an intermediate holding company incorporated in Hong Kong, with supervisory conditions imposed on this intermediate holding company. Accordingly, both financial firms and nonfinancial firms may apply to own and operate a virtual bank in Hong Kong.

322. If an overseas-incorporated virtual bank wishes to establish itself in Hong Kong in branch form, it must come from a country with an established regulatory framework for e-banking; have total assets of more than USD 16 billion and be subject to the 'three-building' condition[323] in respect of its physical offices, but not in respect of its cyber network.

§3. Management and Assessment of Security Aspects of Transactional E-Banking Services

323. To procure security policies, the HKMA issued a Guidance Note in 2000 and updated it in 2011.[324] An updated supervisory policy is now in place.[325] Two parts of security issues are mentioned. When information security is concerned, senior management of authorized institutions should issue and maintain comprehensive information security policies, ensure that they are properly implemented

322. Available at https://www.hkma.gov.hk/media/eng/doc/key-information/guidelines-and-circular/guideline/guideline_eng_virtual_bank_20180608.pdf.
323. Institutions subject to this condition are not allowed to maintain offices in more than three buildings to which customers have access.
324. Management of Security Risks in Electronic Banking Services: A Guidance Note issued by the Monetary Authority, July 2000 (https://www.hkma.gov.hk/eng/regulatory-resources/regulatory-guides/guidelines/2000/07/200007061/).
325. E-banking refers to financial services (which can be transactional, enquiry or payment services) provided to personal or business customers and delivered over the Internet, wireless networks, automatic teller machines (ATMs), fixed telephone networks or other electronic terminals or devices (available at https://www.hkma.gov.hk/media/eng/doc/key-functions/banking-stability/supervisory-policy-manual/TM-E-1.pdf).

and strictly enforced and encourage the development of a security culture in the institution; periodic evaluations of the continued effectiveness of the information security policies and practices should be commissioned. Adequate physical security measures to prevent unauthorized physical access to the critical computer or network equipment of e-banking services shall be implemented.

324. The institutions should put in place adequate security measures, including comprehensive contractual agreements to control the security risks arising from business counterparties and other external parties. Easy-to-understand and prominent advice should be provided to their customers on security precautions in relation to their transactional e-banking services. Adequate measures to detect and record security breaches or weaknesses on an ongoing basis should be implemented, and procedures to report and handle such incidents should be put in place.

325. To procure the system and network security, adequate security measures for their internal networks and network connections to public networks or remote parties should be implemented. The institutions should properly design and configure the servers and firewalls that support and protect their transactional e-banking services – particularly Internet-based e-banking services. The institutions should also implement proper techniques to protect confidentiality of information while it is stored or in passage over external and internal networks; proper techniques to authenticate the identity and authority of their customers and their e-banking systems and to ensure the integrity of information transmitted over networks.

326. For proper assessment of the security aspects, the HKMA further issued a Guidance Note, which guides the senior management of authorized institutions to carry out periodic independent assessments.[326] The independent assessment reports are expected to be submitted to the HKMA for reference. This Guidance Note sets out the expected scope of assessment and provides general guidance on selecting the assessors and on the types of information to be included in the reports.

§4. New Electronic Payment Systems

327. Traditional electronic payment systems such as credit and debit cards have been widely used for many years. These cards have been further adapted for use over the Internet. However, the Internet has led to the emergence of new payment systems. Broadly speaking, there are two types of systems that are used in Hong

326. Independent Assessment of Security Aspects of Transactional E-banking Services: An HKMA Guidance Note, September 2000 (http://www.hkma.gov.hk/eng/key-information/guidelines-and-circulars/guidelines/20000926.shtml).

Kong: Internet-based payment systems and smart cards. The Internet-based payment systems contain a wide variety of types, including the so-called CyberCash,[327] e-Cash and DigiCash.[328]

328. No specific legislation and regulations exist in Hong Kong to deal with the above systems. The HKMA will generally be the body to take on the regulatory task. Some aspects of Internet-based payment systems will also be regulated by the ETO (Cap. 553) and other relevant ordinances such as the Personal Data (Privacy) Ordinance (Cap. 486).

327. For further information, *see* www.paypal.com/cybercash.
328. E-cash is an encrypted electronic payment system which uses the concept of digital coins. Since e-Cash Technologies Inc. purchased the e-Cash system from the DigiCash Inc., e-Cash is sometimes referred to as DigiCash. For further information, *see* C. Wright, et al., *Internet Law in Hong Kong* 213–215 (Sweet & Maxwell 2003).

Chapter 4. Protection of Users of Electronic Services

329. Social unrest in 2019 and the aftermath of the COVID-19 pandemic accelerated online purchases of essential products. As customer traffic and revenue declined, online models have been adopted to connect with customers.

330. According to a Visa Consumer Payment Attitudes Study conducted in August 2020, 52% of Hong Kong purchases were made online during the pandemic, compared to 40% in the pre-COVID-19 period, a trend that is expected to continue beyond the pandemic. The rise of e-commerce has driven the use of credit card payments and alternative payment solutions such as Alipay, PayPal and Google Pay. Thus, how to protect users of electronic services has been rather important to the development of electronic transactions.

331. Consumer confidence is vital to the healthy development of e-commerce. Consumers will at the very least need the same level of protection in cyberspace as they have enjoyed in the physical world. It is a fundamental right that consumers are given appropriate information and assurances on which they can base a decision as to whether they wish to proceed with an online transaction or to view information on a site.[329]

332. Interest groups have claimed a 'consumer bill of rights' for the electronic age to be promulgated, which includes the following:

(a) to be informed of and to validate the identity and location of the organizations offering e-commerce;
(b) to procure authentic products and services as specified in the offerings;
(c) to have a mechanism for redress of problems arising from business transactions;
(d) to be provided with adequate consumer education of their rights in cyberspace; and
(e) to be provided with adequate protection with regard to personal data privacy.[330]

333. Trust Mark Schemes have been launched to give accredited merchants the credibility that consumers are looking for and that address consumer rights.[331] The Hong Kong Consumer Council also has a say in this aspect. It has been a part of the International Marketing Supervision Network (IMSN). Actions are taken to identify dubious websites and collect information on the extent to which consumer rights are

329. P.W.S. Chan, Chief Executive, *Consumer Council, HKSAR* (Consumer Rights and Electronic Commerce 26 Mar. 2001).
330. Electronic Commerce, Consumer Rights and Data Privacy, by S. Lau, *Privacy Commissioner for Personal Data*, Hong Kong at the NetAsia '98, Internet Commerce Expo (ICE) Hong Kong '98, 30 Jul.–1 Aug. 1998, Hong Kong.
331. For example, the online Better Business Bureau and the WebTrust.

not being observed. Such independent assessment can put pressure on relevant websites which shall lose consumers to other traders providing better consumer services.

334. The Customs and Excise Department is the major enforcement agency for consumer protection laws, which include:

- *the Consumer Goods Safety Ordinance*: imposing a statutory duty on manufacturers, importers and suppliers of consumer goods to ensure that the goods they supply for local consumption are reasonably safe;
- *the Toys and Children's Products Safety Ordinance*: imposing a statutory duty on manufacturers, importers and suppliers of toys and children's products to ensure that the goods satisfy the stipulated safety standards;
- *the Unconscionable Contracts Ordinance*: empowering Hong Kong courts to refuse to enforce or to revise unconscionable terms in consumer contracts for the sale of goods or supply of services;
- *the SSITO*: requiring service providers to carry out the services with reasonable care and skill and within a reasonable time;
- *the SGO*: providing an implied condition in the sales of goods that the goods are of merchantable quality and that a buyer has the right to reject defective goods unless he or she has a reasonable opportunity to examine the goods;
- *the Trade Descriptions Ordinance*: prohibiting false trade descriptions, false marks and misstatements in respect of goods, provided in the course of trade;
- *the Weights and Measures Ordinance*: providing rules on units and standards of measurement and weighing or measuring equipment used for trade and regulating trade transactions regarding goods supplied by weight or measure.

335. The laws above are not specifically directed at electronic services; however, they are also applicable to electronic transactions. Another important legal development is the launch of the Unsolicited Electronic Messages Ordinance (Cap. 593) on 1 June 2007, and became fully effective on 22 December 2007. Phase I of the ordinance prohibits the use of unscrupulous techniques to send a large quantity of commercial electronic messages, as well as fraud and other illicit activities related to their multiple sending. Phase II provides an 'opt-out' regime and became effective on 22 December 2007 and updated on 2 February 2012. Rules are established for the sending of commercial electronic messages:

- the sender should not withhold calling line identification information when sending out pre-recorded voice messages or fax messages;
- commercial electronic messages should include accurate sender information;
- commercial electronic messages should provide unsubscribe facility for recipients to opt-out from further messages;
- sending out commercial electronic messages to a recipient after he or she has registered his or her number onto the 'do-not-call' registers for ten working days or longer (except those messages to which consent has been given);

– sending out commercial e-mail messages with misleading subject headings.[332]

This ordinance covers electronic messages including pre-recorded promotional voice messages, fax, e-mail, SMS and MMS messages. The message covered must be for commercial promotional purposes and must have a 'Hong Kong link'. A 'Hong Kong link' means that the message should originate from Hong Kong, or should be authorized to be sent by an individual who is physically present in Hong Kong or a Hong Kong company, or the message is received in Hong Kong or sent to a Hong Kong telephone number.[333]

---

332. Sections 8–13 of the Unsolicited Electronic Messages Ordinance.
333. Section 3 of the Unsolicited Electronic Messages Ordinance.

Part V. Non-contractual Liability

Chapter 1. Negligence

§1. General Introduction

336. Negligence is an act or omission when there is a failure to use ordinary care; it is the failure to do that which a person of ordinary prudence would have done under the same or similar circumstances. Ordinary care means the degree of care that would be used by a person of ordinary prudence under the same or similar circumstances. A business may be liable for negligence if its conduct falls below the standard established by law for protecting others against an unreasonable risk of harm. Businesses are held to the standard of the reasonable business, while professionals in a given business are held to the diligence ordinarily possessed by well-informed members of the trade or profession.[334]

337. The elements of a negligence cause of action are duty of care, breach of a duty of care, proximate cause and damage.[335] Civil liability can result from various activities in the area of ICT. Merchants may create an 'unreasonable risk of harm' in cyberspace engaging in conduct that does not meet industry standards or the standard of exercising reasonable care in the circumstances. For example, third parties can pursue a negligence action against a company that fails to protect confidential information. Liabilities can theoretically arise in almost any country where materials can be downloaded.

§2. Liability for Negligence

338. It should be emphasized that there are rules on limiting liability for negligence in section 7 of the Control of Exemption Clauses Ordinance (Cap. 71). This section provides that there can be no exclusion of liability for death or personal injury. For other losses caused by negligence, a 'reasonableness test' applies. It is not voluntary acceptance of risk simply because a notice or contract term purports to exclude or limit liability for negligence.

339. Several 'reasonableness' guidelines are provided:

334. A. Chiu, et al., *Introduction to Hong Kong Business Law* 219 (Pearson 2001).
335. *See* further D.K. Srivastava ed., *Business Law in Hong Kong*, Ch. 9 (Sweet & Maxwell 2002).

(a) relative strength of bargaining positions and availability of other sources to meet the customer's requirements;
(b) whether the customer received an inducement to agree to the term;
(c) whether the customer knows or can be expected to know of the term by reason of trade usages or previous dealings between the parties;
(d) where the term excludes or restricts any relevant liability if some condition is not complied with, whether it was reasonable at the time of the contract to expect compliance with that condition; and
(e) whether the goods were manufactured, processed or adapted to the special order of the consumer.

340. One important aspect of negligence liability is Internet security. The evolving standard holds a business liable for the failure to implement effective computer systems, as well as for failure to maintain a competent compliance team. The starting point, in this case, is that consultants are expressly or impliedly promising to perform security audits in a diligent and reasonably skilful manner. Failure to maintain the duty to provide protection renders the consultants liable for negligence. Besides inadequate security, a company's exposure to negligence may stem from its website, its online communications or retention of unfit employees.

§3. NEGLIGENT MISSTATEMENTS

341. Statements can be wrong because of negligence. Generally, no recovery will be provided in case of pure economic loss. The main elements for negligent misstatements in the Internet context can be:

(a) assumption of responsibility as the basis for claiming a duty of care;
(b) liability can be imposed even if there is no request for information;
(c) liability can arise even if the defendant does not choose to make the statement but is under a statutory duty to do so or is performing a statutory function in doing so;
(d) the purpose of the statement is to give relevant information, advice or services;
(e) advice must be given in a business or other serious context;
(f) the statement is reasonably relied upon by the plaintiff.[336]

342. The defendant is held liable only when the above elements are present. Nevertheless, in cyberspace, there are very few opportunities for such liability to arise since most websites offer very general information (and often include disclaimers to avoid liability), and the plaintiff might need to obtain further advice to rely upon this general information.[337]

336. *Hedley Byrne v. Heller*, AC 465 (1964).
337. P. Stephenson, A. Kwan & D. Ellis, *Cyberlaw in Hong Kong* 410 (2d ed. LexisNexis 2007).

Chapter 2. Liability of Network Operators

343. Network operators provide the basic facilities for further activities. One of the most widely discussed issues is the liability arising out of copyright, which can be traced to relevant provisions in the Copyright Ordinance. Section 26(4) provides that the mere provision of physical facilities for enabling the making of copies of works to the public does not of itself constitute an act of making available copies of works to the public. Thus, the position of a network operator is defined as the provider of physical facilities, for example, providing wired or wireless transport layers by a telecommunications carrier. As long as the operators work without knowledge of, or have no reason to believe the existence of copyright infringement, the operators shall not be held liable.

344. The ordinance further provides that a copyright is infringed by a person who, without the licence of the copyright owner, transmits the work by means of a telecommunications system (other than by broadcasting or inclusion in a cable programme service) knowing or having reason to believe that infringing copies of the work will be made by means of the reception of the transmission in Hong Kong or elsewhere.[338] According to the definition in the ordinance, 'telecommunications system' means a system for transmitting visual images, sounds or other information by electronic means,[339] so the Internet should also be included.

345. Accordingly, the network operators from which the material was copied may be liable for authorizing the infringement.

346. We must make sure whether support of particular protocols by provision of necessary server software is either 'provision of physical facilities' or 'mere' provision. If the operator assists in providing digital content supplied by other persons, then he or she will run the risk of being liable for both certain types of direct infringement and indirectly liable for 'authorizing' infringements by the other content providers.

347. It is important to note from the Legislative Council Brief that not only ISPs but also operators should be provided with the defence that they should not be held responsible for any article that they were not aware of, or had reasonable grounds for believing it not to be obscene or indecent; or they have had no reasonable opportunity to inspect and had reasonable grounds for believing it not to be obscene or indecent.[340]

338. Section 32(2) of the Copyright Ordinance.
339. Section 198 of the Copyright Ordinance.
340. Legislative Council Brief, Protection of Youth from Obscene and Indecent Materials: The 2000 Review of the Control of Obscene and Indecent Articles Ordinance, File Ref.: ITBB (CR) 8/7/1(00).

Chapter 3. Liability of Service Providers

§1. Regulations on ISPs

348. The ISPs are vital to the normal functioning of the Internet. In Hong Kong, a self-governing body – the HKISPA exists to represent the interests of the ISPs and offers guidance for the practice of the ISPs. The Code of Practice was promulgated in 1997 for voluntary adoption by members of the HKISPA.[341]

349. Having adopted the Code of Practice, members are required to commit to the following practices:

(a) providing good quality services to customers and serving the interests of the public;
(b) complying with all applicable laws and governmental operating guidelines;
(c) cooperating with governmental authorities and authorized organizations;
(d) hosting no illegal content nor facilitating illegal activities knowingly;
(e) educating subscribers and users regarding appropriate online conduct;
(f) making reasonable efforts to investigate any legitimate complaint about any illegal content or activities or any network abuse;
(g) respecting and protecting the privacy of all users.[342]

§2. Liability of ISPs

350. There were heated discussions concerning the service provider's civil liabilities for the making of copies by users of the services or for other acts which constitute an infringement of copyright.[343] The fundamental function of ISPs is to provide access to the Internet. They also usually provide e-mail services, chat rooms or even ICQ platforms. Moreover, most ISPs play the role of Internet Content Providers (ICPs), providing various kinds of information, such as entertainment, shopping, fashion, weather conditions, etc., to users. The ICP's success depends very much on whether its content is interesting enough to attract high hit rates (eyeballs). Some ICPs specialize in one single topic and provide one-stop information search services, which is a natural development in managing infinite information on the Internet.

351. Based on the different services provided, different levels of liabilities can be imposed on ISPs. On 10 July 1996, a public consultation paper was released by an inter-departmental working group to find a way to impose content controls on

341. *See* www.hkispa.org.hk/cop-970410.htm.
342. www.hkispa.org.hk.
343. A. Narayan & L.K. Thakur, *Internet Marketing, E-commerce and Cyber Laws* 272 (Authors Press 2000).

ISPs.[344] The proposals singled out ISPs as the leverage point for exercising control, treating them as analogous to distributors of published magazines. The ISPs would be required to block access to obscene materials and restrict access to indecent materials through the use of a Personal Identification Number (PIN). Strong objections have been voiced regarding the practical feasibility of the proposals. The ISPs view themselves primarily as carriers of information requested by their customers.

352. There is no problem in defining the liability of ISPs regarding their capacity as local hosts for originators of contents. The Copyright Ordinance has actually ruled on this. Section 26(4) precludes the liability of merely providing physical facilities for enabling the making available of copies of works to the public; section 27(4) provides that the person who sent the visual images shall not be regarded as responsible for the infringement; section 65 also protects the act of making a transient and incidental copy which is technically required for viewing or listening to the work by a member of the public to whom a copy of the work is made available.

353. Furthermore, section 205(4) states that the mere provision of physical facilities for enabling the making available to the public copies of a fixation of a performance does not of itself constitute an act of making available to the public copies of fixations.[345] The ISPs would not be ready to undertake the arduous task of classifying obscene and indecent materials. The ISPs expressed their willingness to set up an industry association but declined the quasi-regulatory power the government wanted them to have.[346]

§3. Liability of ISPs in Case of Defamation

354. The Defamation Ordinance was enacted before the information age; however, section 25, dealing with unintentional defamation by publishers, can be used to exemplify this issue for ISPs. The relevant provisions can be perfectly applied to ISPs. If an ISP unintentionally publishes a page containing defamatory words, the ISP can make an 'offer of amends', which includes placing a sufficient apology on the ISP's home page for a certain period of time. Section 25(1)(a) provides that if the offer of amends is accepted, no proceedings for libel or slander shall be undertaken by the plaintiff or intended plaintiff against the ISPs, but this does not apply to the author of the words or any other person deemed responsible for the transmission.

355. Nevertheless, when the offer of amends is not accepted, the ISPs can provide a defence that the words complained of were published innocently and that the

344. Regulation of Obscene and Indecent Materials Transmitted through the Internet: Consultation Paper, Hong Kong Government, Broadcasting, Culture and Sport Branch, 10 Jul. 1996, LegCo Paper No. CB(2) 1030/96-97.
345. Section 205(4) of the Copyright Ordinance.
346. M. Mueller, *Telecom Policy and Digital Convergence: The Hong Kong Economic Policy Studies Series* 48–50 (City U.H.K. Press 1997).

offer was made as soon as practicable after the defendant received notice of defamation. While providing the basic liability for ISPs, section 25 further defines the form and content of the offer of amends and the requirements for a valid offer of amends.

356. Section 25(5) defines the situation for innocent publications: the ISP did not intend to publish them of and concerning that other person, and did not know of circumstances by virtue of which they might be understood to refer to him or her; or the words were not defamatory on the face of them, and the ISP did not know of circumstances by virtue of which they might be understood to be defamatory of that person, and in either case that the ISP exercised all reasonable care in relation to the publication; and any reference to the ISP shall be construed as including a reference to any servant or agent of his who was concerned with the contents of the publication.

357. The ambiguous provision contained in this subsection caused some problems as discussed above. For example, there shall be diverse understandings on 'reasonable care'. Thus, when applying this ordinance in discussing the liability of ISPs, we should take notice of the development of practice and attitudes in this area. Relevant cases have been decided in Hong Kong concerning disclosure of information regarding the maker of defamatory statements: ISPs were ordered to provide the IP address of the author of the defamatory statement.[347]

§4. Liability of ISPs in Case of Obscene and Indecent Articles

358. The Control of Obscene and Indecent Articles Ordinance clearly subjects ISPs to liability for transmission of obscene and indecent articles provided by others. Section 21 clearly holds a person liable for publishing such articles. The ISPs can only plead innocence in relation to possession and importation. In such cases, the ISPs must prove that at the time of the alleged offence the article was for the purpose of submission to the Registrar of the High Court or by a person licensed under the Broadcasting Ordinance (Cap. 562) for the purpose of submission under that ordinance. The ISP can also raise the defence that it had no reasonable opportunity to inspect the article and had reasonable grounds for believing that the article was not obscene.[348]

359. The HKSAR Government and the HKISPA have jointly developed a Code of Practice: Practice Statement on Regulation of Obscene and Indecent Material, which was formulated on the basis of the Control of Obscene and Indecent Articles Ordinance. This Code was promulgated in October 1997. The ISPs are expected to

347. *E-Silkroad Holdings Ltd. & Others v. Icered.com Ltd.* HCA 1321/2001; *Max Loh Khum Whai v. Icered Ltd.* HCMP 275/2002.

348. Section 21(c) and (d) of the Control of Obscene and Indecent Articles Ordinance.

take reasonable steps to prevent users of their services from placing obscene materials on the Internet or transmitting such materials using the Internet and inform users not to publish or make available indecent materials to persons under the age of 18 years.[349]

360. As recognized, it is not reasonable to expect ISPs, as conveyors of information to screen, to be cognizant of all the information that may be uploaded onto or downloaded from the Internet by users or that may be transmitted to and from their server by other servers on the Internet. Thus, it is proposed that ISPs should be provided with a defence against articles they are not aware of or have reasonable grounds for believing such articles not to be obscene or indecent.

361. Accordingly, the proposal to clarify the liabilities of ISPs is as follows:

(a) if an ISP is aware of or has been notified that a user of its services has placed obscene articles on the Internet to which the public has access, it must take prompt action to remove or block access to the obscene articles; and
(b) if an ISP is aware of or has been notified that a user of its services has placed indecent articles on the Internet to which the public has access, it must promptly ask the user to post an on-screen forewarning indicating that the article contains material which may offend and may not be published for a person under the age of 18. If the user fails to post the warning notice within a specified period, the ISP must block access to the offensive articles or cease to provide services to the user.[350]

362. This is also in accordance with the Code of Practice for ISPs. The ISP should inform its users not to place on the Internet or transmit material likely to be obscene. In case of being aware that obscene or indecent materials have been placed on the Internet or transmitted, the ISP shall be deemed to have performed its task, if it:

(a) promptly blocks access to the website or database containing obscene material or advises the user to place a warning notice;
(b) promptly informs the user about the possible offence or breach of the subscriber's service conditions;
(c) promptly cancels the account of any subscriber that repeats the offending conduct despite being informed of the contents in (b);
(d) reports to the HKISPA on action taken listed above.[351]

---

349. Articles 5 and 7 of the Code of Practice: Practice Statement on Regulation of Obscene and Indecent Material.
350. Legislative Council Brief, Protection of Youth from Obscene and Indecent Materials: The 2000 Review of the Control of Obscene and Indecent Articles Ordinance, File Ref.: ITBB (CR) 8/7/1(00).
351. Articles 9 and 10 of the Code of Practice: Practice Statement on Regulation of Obscene and Indecent Material.

363. The ISP shall be liable for failing to perform the above tasks. Other than the liability to be imposed based on the Control of Obscene and Indecent Articles Ordinance, the ISP can be subject to any disciplinary actions by the HKISPA for breach of the Practice Statement.

Chapter 4. Product Liability

364. Product liability is the legal liability of manufacturers for injuries caused by the marketing of defective products. The Consumer Goods Safety Ordinance (Cap. 456) provides the basic framework for product liability in Hong Kong. The ordinance imposes a duty on manufacturers, importers and suppliers of certain consumer products to ensure the safety of consumer goods.

365. The application of the ordinance is limited to consumer goods, not including electrical goods. No distinction has been made between a party dealing as a final consumer and a party dealing in the course of business. The ordinance provides that a person shall not supply, manufacture or import consumer goods into Hong Kong unless they comply with either the general safety requirement for consumer goods or any applicable approved standard for the particular consumer goods.[352]

366. The general safety requirement for consumer goods is that the goods are reasonably safe under all of the circumstances, including:

(a) the manner in which and the purpose for which the consumer goods are presented, promoted or marketed;
(b) the use of any mark in relation to the consumer goods and instructions or warnings;
(c) reasonable safety standards published by a standard institute or similar body for consumer goods of the description which applies; and
(d) the existence of any reasonable means (taking into account the cost, likelihood and extent of any improvement) to make the consumer goods safer.[353]

367. Violation of the ordinance will constitute an offence and certain penalties are provided including fines and imprisonment.

368. Other relevant ordinances also apply to labelling requirements of consumer goods and indecent articles,[354] but they are not directed specifically to e-commerce; thus are not included in the present discussion.

369. The product in the transaction can be content. Content owners might need to ensure that the end-users of their works observe any requirements that the content owners impose on the use of the works, including payment conditions. Owners might also need to enforce these conditions against other users such as illegal copiers and borrowers. Content owners also need to ensure that those who distribute their content do not distribute pirate copies or do anything that interferes with their content protection measures.

352. Section 6 of the Consumer Goods Safety Ordinance.
353. Section 4(1) of the Consumer Goods Safety Ordinance.
354. For example, the Toys and Children Products Safety Ordinance.

370. The same liability can arise for the content owner who has to ensure that he or she is the owner of the content; violation of this warranty can subject the content provider to contractual liability and even criminal liability.

Part VI. Privacy Protection

Chapter 1. Regulation of Personal Data Processing

§1. Personal Data (Privacy) Ordinance

371. It is widely recognized that technological development has facilitated collection, holding, manipulation, disclosure and transfer of vast amounts of personal data, which have put individuals' privacy at risk.

372. The Personal Data (Privacy) Ordinance is the most important document in protecting personal privacy by regulating the collection and use of personal data relating to living individuals by businesses in Hong Kong.[355] It came into force on 20 December 1996 aiming to protect the individual's right to privacy with respect to personal data. It also safeguards the flow of personal data to Hong Kong from countries that already have such laws.

373. This ordinance is very broad in its scope and provides a great level of protection of personal data. The ordinance covers any data relating directly or indirectly to a living individual (data subject), from which it is practicable to directly or indirectly ascertain the identity of the individual and which are in a form in which access or processing is practicable.[356] Data relating to an anonymous subject which the data user does not seek to identify does not amount to personal data.[357] Without differentiating personal data according to its sensitivity, it applies to any person (data user) who holds or processes another person's personal data or uses it solely on behalf of the second-mentioned person.[358] The most important part of the ordinance consists of six data protection principles, encompassing a set of fair information practices that have achieved international acceptance.

374. The ordinance requires that the collection of personal data be lawful and fair in the circumstances of the case. It provides that all practicable steps must be taken to ensure that the data subject is explicitly or implicitly informed on or before collecting the data for the designated purpose, and is explicitly informed of the

355. Personal Data (Privacy) Ordinance, Cap. 486, 30 Jun. 1997. *See* generally M. Berthold & R. Wacks, *Data Privacy Law in Hong Kong* (FT Law & Tax 1997).
356. Section 2 of the Personal Data (Privacy) Ordinance.
357. *Easterweek Publisher Ltd. & Another v. Privacy Commissioner for Personal Data* [2000] 1 HKC 692.
358. Section 2(12) of the Personal Data (Privacy) Ordinance.

classes of persons to whom the data may be transferred (so that the individual can decide whether to provide the data).[359] All practicable steps must be taken to ensure that personal data is protected against unauthorized or accidental access, processing, erasure, loss or other use.[360] Data subjects should have rights of access to and collection of their personal data.[361] Personal data must not, without the consent of the data subject, be used for a new purpose.[362] Individuals have privacy interests in their personal information, and those interests must be respected and protected.[363]

375. The key message from the data protection principles is that persons who collect, use, hold and process personal information need to develop a special sensitivity towards such information. Personal information must not be treated as being simply a commercial commodity or just a tool of trade. Individuals have privacy interests in their personal information, and those interests must be respected and protected.[364]

376. The ordinance further provides specific exemptions from the requirements of the ordinance, which include:

(a) a broad exemption from the provisions of the ordinance for personal data held for domestic or recreational purposes;
(b) exemptions from the requirements on subject access for certain employment-related personal data; and
(c) exemptions from the subject access and use limitation requirements of the ordinance where their application is likely to prejudice certain competing public or social interests, such as: security, defence and international relations; prevention or detection of crime; assessment or collection of any tax or duty; news activities; and health.

§2. The Privacy Commissioner for Personal Data

377. The Privacy Commissioner for Personal Data was appointed to ensure the enforcement of this ordinance.[365] The Commissioner is appointed by the Chief Executive by notice in the *Gazette*. The Office of the Privacy Commissioner is an independent regulatory organization headed by the Commissioner. A Deputy Privacy Commissioner assists the Commissioner in the overall administration and strategic planning. A Personal Data (Privacy) Advisory Committee was established under the ordinance to advise the Commissioner on matters relevant to the privacy

359. Data Protection Principles, Sch. 1, Principle 1 – purpose and manner of collection of personal data.
360. *Ibid.*, Principle 4 – security of personal data.
361. *Ibid.*, Principle 6 – access to personal data.
362. *Ibid.*, Principle 3 – use of personal data.
363. R. McLeish, *Deputy Privacy Commissioner for Personal Data, Getting to Know the Personal Data (Privacy) Ordinance* (available at https://www.pcpd.org.hk/english/news_events/speech/speech_19970300.html).
364. *Ibid.*
365. *See* Privacy Commissioner, First Annual Report 1996–1997.

of individuals in relation to personal data. In 2014–2015, the Office had a total of eighty-two staff divided into seven divisions.[366]

378. His or her duties and powers include:

(a) monitoring and supervising compliance with the provisions of the ordinance;
(b) promoting and assisting bodies representing data users to prepare codes of practice in compliance with the principles of the ordinance;
(c) promoting the awareness and understanding of the ordinance's requirements;
(d) examining any proposed legislation that affects the privacy of individuals and providing feedback to the proposers;
(e) undertaking research on any likely adverse effects of any process has on the privacy of individuals;
(f) Liaising and cooperating with any person outside Hong Kong to better perform above function;
(g) inspecting personal data systems and making recommendations for compliance with provisions of the ordinance.[367]

379. Failure to comply with the principles above shall not automatically constitute an offence. However, the Commissioner may serve an enforcement notice on a data user in the event of such a breach. Failure to enforce the notice from the Commissioner shall subject the data user to a fine at Level 5 (at present HKD 25,001 to HKD 50,000) and imprisonment for two years or to a daily penalty in case of a continuing offence.

380. Anyone suffering from damage, including injured feelings, as a result of the contravention of the ordinance in relation to his or her personal data may submit a complaint. As defined in section 37, a complaint must satisfy the following conditions:

(a) it is in respect of an act or practice of a data user specified in the complaint, which relates to personal data;
(b) the complaint is brought by the individual who is the subject of the data or by someone else in the capacity of a relevant person of such individual as defined in the ordinance; and
(c) the act or practice may be a contravention of a requirement under the ordinance.

381. Failing to satisfy the conditions above, the case shall not be treated as a complaint. However, where the Commissioner has reasonable grounds to believe that there may have been contravention of a requirement of the ordinance which

366. Annual Report 2014–2015, Office of the Privacy Commissioner for Personal Data (available at https://www.pcpd.org.hk/english/resources_centre/publications/annual_report/files/anreport15_01.pdf).
367. Section 8(1) of the Personal Data (Privacy) Ordinance.

involves personal data other than that of the complainant, he or she may commence an investigation into the matter on his or her own initiative under paragraph (b) and (ii) of section 38.

382. The Commissioner may issue codes of conduct to provide guidance on compliance with the ordinance's necessarily general provisions. So far, several important codes have been issued, including the code on the use of personal identifiers[368] and of credit information,[369] Code of Practice on Consumer Credit Data (revised in January 2013), Code of Practice on the Identity Card Number and Other Personal Identifiers (revised in January 2016), and Privacy Guidelines: Monitoring and Personal Data Privacy at Work (revised in April 2016).

§3. Data User Returns and Register of Data Users

383. A data user shall submit to the Commissioner a data user return:[370]

(a) in the specified form;
(b) containing the prescribed information required by the return in relation to the data user;
(c) in the case of:
   (i) a data user who belongs to the class of data users concerned on the day on which the notice specifying that class commences, not earlier than three months before, and not later than each anniversary of that day;
   (ii) a data user who first belongs to the class of data users concerned in a day after the day on which the notice specifying that class commences, not earlier than three months before, and not later than each anniversary of that first-mentioned day.
(d) accompanied by the prescribed fee.[371]

384. The Commissioner should use the data user return and any notices served on him or her to keep and maintain a register of data users who have submitted such returns.[372] The register shall be in the form of a database and contain, in respect of each data user who has submitted a data user return, such particulars of the information supplied in that return as the Commissioner thinks fit.[373]

---

368. The Code of Practice on the Identity Card Number and other Personal Identifiers were published in the *Gazette* on 19 Dec. 1997. With the exception of the requirement restricting the issue of a card with an identity card number printed on it, the requirements of the Code took effect on 19 Jun. 1998.
369. The Code of Practice on Consumer Credit Data was first issued on 27 Feb. 1998 and revised in June 2003 (available at www.pco.org.uk).
370. Data User Returns refer to declaration forms to be completed by data users concerning their basic information.
371. Section 14(4) of the Personal Data (Privacy) Ordinance.
372. Section 15(1) of the Personal Data (Privacy) Ordinance.
373. Section 15(2) of the Personal Data (Privacy) Ordinance.

385. Furthermore, the Commissioner shall provide facilities for making the particulars contained in the register available for inspection:

(a) by any person;
(b) in visible and legible form;
(c) during ordinary office hours; and
(d) free of charge.[374]

§4. Access to and Correction of Personal Data

386. An individual may request to be informed by a data user whether the data user holds personal data of which the individual is the data subject or to be supplied by the data user with a copy of such data if the user holds such data.[375] A data user should comply with a data access request not later than forty days after receiving the request. In the case of failing to comply, the data user shall:

(a) before the expiration of that period:
  (i) by notice in writing, inform the requestor that the data user is unable to comply and the reasons why; and
  (ii) comply with the request to the extent, if any, that the data user is able to do so.
(b) as soon as practicable after the expiration of that period, comply or fully comply, as the case may be, with the request.[376]

387. A data user can further refuse to comply with a data access request under certain circumstances, which can be found in section 21(1) and (2) of the Personal Data (Privacy) Ordinance. An individual or relevant person may make a request that the data user make the necessary correction to the data if a copy of the personal data has been supplied by a data user in compliance with a data access request and the person who considers that the data is inaccurate makes a request for correction.[377]

§5. Matching Procedures and Transfer of Information

388. Matching procedures refer to any procedures whereby personal data collected for one or more purposes in respect of ten or more data subjects are compared (except for manual means) with personal data collected for any other purpose in respect of those data subjects where the comparison:

(a) is (whether in whole or in part) for the purpose of producing or verifying data; or

374. Section 16(1) of the Personal Data (Privacy) Ordinance.
375. Section 18(1) of the Personal Data (Privacy) Ordinance.
376. Section 19(1)(2) of the Personal Data (Privacy) Ordinance.
377. Section 22(1) of the Personal Data (Privacy) Ordinance.

(b) produces or verifies data in respect of which it is reasonable to believe that it is practicable that the data may be used (whether immediately or at any subsequent time) for the purpose of taking adverse action against any of those data subjects.[378]

389. A matching procedure is not necessary:

(a) unless and until each individual who is a data subject of the personal data which is the subject of that procedure has given his or her prescribed consent to the procedure being carried out;
(b) unless and until the Commissioner has consented to the procedure being carried out;
(c) unless the procedure:
  (i) belongs to a class of matching procedures specified in a notice; and
  (ii) is carried out in accordance with the conditions, if any, specified in the notice.
(d) unless it is required or permitted under any provision of any ordinance specified.[379]

390. Section 33 of the ordinance rules on the transfer of information outside Hong Kong through the Internet: a data user shall not transfer personal data to a place outside Hong Kong unless:

(a) the place is specified for the purpose of this section in a notice;
(b) the user has reasonable grounds for believing that there is in force in that place any law which is substantially similar to, or serves the same purposes as, this ordinance;
(c) the data subject has consented in writing to the transfer;
(d) the user has reasonable grounds for believing that, in all the circumstances of the case:
  (i) the transfer is for the avoidance or mitigation of adverse action against the data subject;
  (ii) it is not practicable to obtain the consent in writing of the data subject to that transfer; and
  (iii) if it was practicable to obtain such consent, the data subject would give it.
(e) the data is exempt from data protection principle 3 by virtue of an exemption under Part 8;
(f) the user has taken reasonable precautions and exercised all due diligence to ensure that the data will not, in that place, be collected, held, processed or used in any manner which, if that place were in Hong Kong, would be a contravention of a requirement under this ordinance.[380]

---

378. Section 2 of Personal Data (Privacy) Ordinance.
379. Section 30(1) of the Personal Data (Privacy) Ordinance.
380. Section 33(2)(f) of the Personal Data (Privacy) Ordinance.

391. The ordinance further provides rules on legitimate use of personal data in case of direct marketing. A data user who has obtained personal data from any source and uses the data for direct marketing purposes, must:

- inform the data subject that the data users intend to so use the personal data and that the data users may not so use the data unless the data user has received the data subject's consent to the intended use;
- provides the data subject the kinds of personal data to be used and the classes of marketing subjects; and
- provide the data subject with a channel through which the data subject may, without charge by the data user, communicate the data subject's consent to the intended use.[381]

392. For the purpose of this provision, 'direct marketing' means: the offering of goods, facilities or services; the advertising of the availability of goods, facilities or services; or the solicitation of donations or contributions for charitable, cultural, philanthropic, recreational, political or other purposes, by means of telephone calls made to specific persons or information or goods sent to any person by mail, facsimile transmission, e-mail or other similar means of communication, where the information or goods are addressed to specific persons.[382]

§6. Transparency of the Policy on Personal Data Privacy

393. There are several means to make the above ordinance transparent to the public:[383]

(a) Avoid the web façade. Provide web pages that make available information 'About the Organization', including the name, physical location and contact telephone/fax numbers of the organization in addition to the web address or e-mail address. This would be a reliable channel through which a web user could contact the organization.
(b) Make the privacy policy statement easy to access. One possible method is to set up the privacy policy statement as a linked page accessible from the home page or other pages where personal data are collected, for example, a registration page where registration is required for access or a customer agreement page.
(c) State the privacy policy clearly, which should inform the web users of the kinds of personal data held by the organization and the main purposes for which the personal data are used or are to be used.
(d) Provide a Personal Information Collection statement, to inform a person from whom personal data are requested on how these data are to be used, to whom

381. Section 35(C) of the Personal Data (Privacy) Ordinance.
382. Section 35(A) of the Personal Data (Privacy) Ordinance.
383. This part is based on A Guide to Personal Data Privacy and Consumer Protection on the Internet, published by Hong Kong Productivity Council, also (available at www.hkispa.org.hk/pdf/guide-e.pdf).

they may be transferred, and the person's rights to request a copy of the data and correct any errors and who should be contacted to make such requests.

394. Furthermore, several guidelines are provided to help the public adopt appropriate means to protect their own privacy, namely:

(a) collect adequate but not excessive data relevant to the purpose, for example, if no purchase is to be made, generally it will be excessive and not relevant to request a credit card number;
(b) state whether personal data will be displayed at the time of collection. If personal details are collected and are later to be displayed on the Internet or elsewhere this intention must be made clear to the individual or elsewhere; this intention must be made clear to the individual at the time of collecting the data;
(c) ensure anonymity of personal data when displaying them on the Internet as an additional precautionary step to avoid presenting detailed information that might be excessive or abused;
(d) use encryption when transmitting sensitive personal data to reduce the risk of this information being used by other people;
(e) provide a privacy warning message if unencrypted data transfer is used for the transmission by users of sensitive personal data;
(f) use of 'clicktrail' information. An ISP should not use the 'clicktrail' information to analyse a customer's interests as the data are not provided for such purposes;
(g) offer a secure environment that meets service commitment as the ISP has the liability to protect customers' sensitive information from unauthorized access or hacker attacks.[384]

§7. Complaint Handling Policy

395. An individual, or a relevant person on behalf of an individual, may make a complaint to the Commissioner about an act or practice:

(a) specified in the complaint; and
(b) that:
  (i) has been done or engaged in, or is being done or engaged in, as the case may be, by a data user specified in the complaint;
  (ii) relates to personal data of which the individual is or, in any case in which the data user is relying upon an exemption, may be the data subject; and
  (iii) may be a contravention of a requirement under this ordinance.[385]

384. The information is provided by the Office of the Privacy Commissioner for Personal Data, Hong Kong (available at www.pco.org.hk).
385. Section 37(1) of the Personal Data (Privacy) Ordinance.

396. The purpose of the policy is:

(a) in the case of a complaint under section 37 of the ordinance, to bring to the awareness of the relevant parties the standard policy of the Privacy Commissioner's Office (PCO) in handling such complaint to enable them to have a basic understanding and realistic expectation of how their case is to be handled; and
(b) in the event of any subsequent appeal to the Administrative Appeals Board, to enable the board to give regard to such policy in accordance with section 21(2) of the Administrative Appeals Board Ordinance.

397. The policy covers the handling by the PCO of any complaint under section 37 of the ordinance, including but not limited to the following:

(a) receiving a complaint under section 37;
(b) discretion under section 39(2) to refuse to carry out or continue an investigation;
(c) exercising the general powers of investigation under Part VII; and
(d) issuing an enforcement notice under section 50.

Chapter 2. Protection of Telecommunications Privacy

398. Under the common law, one who intentionally intrudes, physically or otherwise, upon the solitude or seclusion of another or his or her private affairs or concerns is subject to liability to the other for invasion of his or her privacy, if the intrusion would be highly offensive to a reasonable person.[386] Four kinds of interests are protected by a person's right to privacy: unreasonable intrusions upon the seclusion of another; appropriation of the other's name or likeness; unreasonable publicity given to the other's private life; and publicity that unreasonably places the other in a false light before the public.[387]

399. The Basic Law of the HKSAR contains several articles on privacy protection. Article 30 has close connections with telecommunications. It provides that the freedom and privacy of communications of Hong Kong residents shall be protected by law. No department or individual may, on any grounds, infringe upon the freedom and privacy of communications of residents except that the relevant authorities may inspect communications in accordance with legal procedures to meet the needs of public security or of investigations into criminal offences.

400. With this provision as guidance, further actions were carried out, in addition to the Personal Data (Privacy) Ordinance. With regard to two cases related to unauthorized disclosure of telecom subscriber data to debt collectors,[388] Hong Kong's Independent Commission Against Corruption (ICAC) issued a study which called for closer cooperation among the government agencies responsible for telecommunications in Hong Kong.[389]

401. In June 2002, the Privacy Commissioner jointly launched a voluntary Code of Practice on Protection of Customer Information for Fixed and Mobile Service Operators (Code) with Hong Kong's Consumer Council, the ICAC and the OFTA.[390] This Code is the result of efforts to bring the privacy rules for telecommunication companies into one document.

402. The Code covers five areas, namely: policy on protection of customer personal data; technical measures for protection of customer personal data; location security; staff security; and transfer of customer personal data.[391] Although the areas are more or less still concerned with personal data, the emphasis of the Code is on the service providers.

386. S.D. Warren & L.D. Brandeis, *The Right to Privacy*, 4 Harv. L. Rev. 193 (1890).
387. Restatement (Second) of Torts, s. 652 A (1965).
388. S. Schwartz, *Phone Firms Urged to Adopt Pioneering Data Privacy Code* 4 (South China Morning Post June 2002).
389. Four Hong Kong Government Agencies Issue New Privacy Guidelines for Telecom Industry, BNA Privacy Law Watch, 21 Jun. 2002.
390. Privacy Commissioner for Personal Data, Press Release, New Code Launched for Fixed and Mobile Service Operators to Protect Customer Information, 17 Jun. 2002.
391. Privacy Commissioner for Personal Data, Code of Practice on Protection of Customer Information for Fixed and Mobile Service Operators 3–4 (Hong Kong, PCO, 2002).

Part VII. Computer-Related Crime

Chapter 1. General Legal Development

403. Computers have become an inseparable part of most people's daily lives. While offering efficient services, computers also give rise to new forms of crimes. Many crimes are simply traditional crimes, committed with an innovative tool – the computer, which include computer hardware and chip theft, unauthorized access, virus infection, intellectual property theft, theft of services, invasion of privacy, embezzlement, forgery and fraud, pornography, money laundering, extortion, espionage and terrorism. A variety of free electronic programmes have been available on the Internet to disseminate knowledge on how to become 'hackers' and 'crackers'. Only the latter are genuine computer crimes.[392] In Hong Kong, there have been reported cases on unauthorized access,[393] simple theft and fraud.

404. Criminal legislation is territorial in nature, which means, such a rule shall be valid over the acts conducted within a specific area. Criminal activities arise along with the wide use of the Internet. Typical examples include: unauthorized access with intention to commit offences such as Internet fraud, theft or misappropriation of information relating to intellectual property rights; hacking; destruction of digital information through the use of viruses and logic bombs; and harmful sites and contents on the Internet.[394]

405. Long ago, the HKSAR Government recognized the possibility of criminal activities concerning the abusive use of the Internet. The Computer Crimes Ordinance was enacted in 1993 to deal with damage to computer systems and data. It has, through amending the Telecommunications Ordinance (Cap. 106), Crimes Ordinance (Cap. 200) and Theft Ordinance (Cap. 210), created new offences. Nevertheless, the offences then created or expanded are still able to catch most types of reported computer crimes.

---

392. The Hong Kong government has been able to split computer crime into two distinct categories: crimes targeted at the computer or computer system (such as hacking or the disseminating of computer viruses); and crimes using the computer as a medium (such as for the purpose of gambling or viewing/posting child pornography). P. Stephenson, et al., *Cyberlaw in Hong Kong* 101 (2d ed. Lexis Nexis 2007).
393. *HKSAR v. Tam Hei Lun & Others* [2000] 768 HKCU 1; *HKSAR v. Ko Kam Fai* [2001] 3 HKC 181.
394. A. Edappagath & E. Kim, *Legal and Regulatory Awareness of the ICT-Identifying Solutions for Cybercrimes* 2 (Business Briefing: Global Infosecurity 2002).

406. Witnessing the rapid development of the Internet, the HKSAR Government set up an inter-departmental working group under the Security Bureau in March 2000 to study the new issues so that the measures taken shall not lag behind. The issues examined include identifying problems and recommending solutions, legislative or otherwise, regarding crime prevention, evidence gathering, investigation and prosecution arising from computer crimes.[395] The first report was published on 1 December 2000 for public consultation, which lasted until 28 February 2001. After receiving comments from interested groups,[396] this report largely improves the general understanding of computer crimes in Hong Kong and fine-tunes responses to the government.

407. The Hong Kong Police have been performing an important role in curbing computer crimes. A Computer Crime Section was set up in 1993 to investigate complaints of computer crime at the central level. This was followed by dedicated resources for preventing computer crime and increasing the capability of handling computer crime on the front lines. The Computer Crime Section was expanded in 2001 to become a sophisticated Technology Crime Division, which pool and enhance police expertise in computer crime investigations, host a computer forensics laboratory and maintain close liaison with international law enforcement agencies.[397]

395. The report is (available at www.hkispa.org.hk/pdf/ComputerRelatedCrime.pdf).
396. *See*, e.g., Comment and Recommendation to the Inter-departmental Working Group on Computer Related Crime Report, by C. Soong, *Chairman of the HKISPA*, LC Paper No. CB(2)811/00-01(01).
397. www.police.gov.hk/ppp_en/04_crime_matters/tcd/tcd.html.

Chapter 2. Application of Substantive Criminal Law in the Area of ICT

408. In Hong Kong, activities concerning computer content and information are highlighted for possible liability. The Crimes Ordinance (Cap. 200) is formulated to deal with criminal matters in general. However, several sections have been formulated to deal specifically with computers and information. Section 59(1)(b) defines 'property' to include any program or data, held in a computer or in a computer storage medium, whether or not the program or data is a property of tangible nature. Thus, the ordinance clearly includes the area of ICT within its regulatory scope. Section 59 further clarifies that 'to destroy or damage any property' in relation to a computer includes the misuse of a computer.

409. According to this section, 'misuse of a computer' means:

(a) to cause a computer to function other than as it has been established to function by or on behalf of its owner, notwithstanding that the misuse may not impair the operation of the computer or a program held in the computer or the reliability of data held in the computer;
(b) to alter or erase any program or data held in a computer or in a computer storage medium;
(c) to add any program or data to the contents of a computer or of a computer storage medium; and
(d) any act which contributes towards causing the misuse of a kind referred to in paragraph (a), (b) or (c) shall be regarded as causing it.

410. Section 161 provides that any person who gains access to a computer with intent to commit an offence, or with a dishonest intent to deceive, or with a view to dishonest gain for himself or herself or another, or with a dishonest intent to cause loss to another shall be deemed to commit an offence. The provisions in the Crimes Ordinance offer the basic framework for further legislation. Several areas have been regulated later by specific ordinances.

§1. Obscene and Indecent Content

411. Under the Control of Obscene and Indecent Articles Ordinance (Cap. 390), it is an offence to publish an obscene article (whether or not the person knows the article is obscene); to publish an indecent article to a person under the age of 18 years; to publicly display any indecent matter (whether or not the person knows the matter is indecent) or to publish certain other kinds of classified articles without the required warnings.[398] The ordinance aims at regulating the content of published articles.

398. Sections 21–23 of the Control of Obscene and Indecent Articles Ordinance.

412. Generally speaking, this ordinance also regulates content published via the Internet. The term 'article' refers to anything consisting of or containing: material to be read or looked at, or both; any sound recording; and any film, videotape, disc or other recordings of a picture, or pictures.[399] Thus, materials displayed on the Internet shall be included in this interpretation.

413. The ordinance was passed in 1987 following a strong demand for a crackdown on pornographic publications. The Obscene Articles Tribunal (OAT) was set up for this purpose. It is a judicial body and enjoys exclusive jurisdiction in determining the obscenity or indecency of an article.

414. An object is obscene if, by reason of obscenity, it is not suitable to be published for any person; an object is indecent if, by reason of indecency, it is not suitable to be published for a juvenile. Both 'obscenity' and 'indecency' include violence, depravity and repulsiveness. A person can be liable for distributing, circulating, selling, hiring, giving or lending an article to the public or a section of the public, whether or not for gain.[400]

415. Liability can also be imposed when any matter is displayed in or is visible from any place to which the public has or is permitted to have access, whether upon payment or otherwise. Such a display shall, for the purpose of this ordinance, be deemed to be publicly displayed. An exception is provided if displayed in a place to which the public is permitted access only upon payment which is for or includes payment for a display of indecent matter.[401]

416. Several guidelines are provided to determine obscene and indecent articles:

(a) standards of morality, decency and propriety that are generally accepted by reasonable members of the community, and in relation thereto may, in the case of an article, have regard to any decision of a censor under section 10 of the Film Censorship Ordinance (Cap. 392) in respect of a film within the meaning of section 2(1) of that ordinance;
(b) the dominant effect of an article or of matter as a whole;
(c) in the case of an article, the persons or class of persons or age groups of persons, to or among whom the article is, or is intended, or is likely to be published;
(d) in the case of matter publicly displayed, the location where the matter is or is to be publicly displayed and the persons or class of persons or age groups of persons likely to view such matter; and
(e) whether the article or matter has an honest purpose or whether its content is merely camouflage designed to render acceptable any part of it.[402]

399. Section 2(1) of the Control of Obscene and Indecent Articles Ordinance.
400. Section 2(2)–(4) of the Control of Obscene and Indecent Articles Ordinance.
401. Section 2(7) of the Control of Obscene and Indecent Articles Ordinance.
402. Section 10(1) of the Control of Obscene and Indecent Articles Ordinance.

417. The author, printer, manufacturer, publisher, importer, distributor or owner of the copyright of any article or any person who commissions the design, production or publication of any article may, by application in the prescribed form, submit that article to the Registrar for classification by a tribunal. They must give notice of any such classification in a prescribed manner. The Secretary for Justice and any public officer authorized in that regard by the Chief Secretary for Administration can also apply for classification.[403]

418. Articles considered to be 'indecent' by the OAT may not be distributed to a person under 18 years of age and must carry a prescribed on-screen warning on the web page which must be clearly and conspicuously displayed before indecent content can be reviewed. The prescribed warning is as follows:

Warning: this article contains material which may offend and may not be distributed, circulated, sold, hired, given, lent, shown, played or projected to a person under the age of 18 years.

419. Any person who publishes possesses for the purpose of publication or imports for the purpose of publication, any obscene article, whether or not he or she knows that it is an obscene article, commits an offence and is liable to a fine of HKD 1 million and to imprisonment for three years.[404]

420. The government has increasingly attempted to use this ordinance to meet the content regulation challenges posed by new telecommunication media. The Practice Statement on the Regulation of Obscene and Indecent Material (Statement) provides certain recommendations and guidelines for members of the HKISPA in relation to obscene and indecent materials transmitted over the Internet.[405] In order to meet the requirements of the statement, a member of the HKISPA must require users not to place on the Internet or transmit material likely to be classified as obscene under the ordinance. Where a member becomes aware that a user has placed indecent material on the Internet or has transmitted indecent material over the Internet without putting up a warning notice, the member must promptly:

- request the user to put up such a warning notice;
- inform the user that he or she may be committing an offence under the ordinance and is in breach of the member's terms and conditions;
- cancel the account of any user who repeatedly places indecent material on the Internet or transmits it over the Internet; and
- report the matter to the HKISPA.[406]

403. Sections 13 and 18 of the Control of Obscene and Indecent Articles Ordinance.
404. Section 21(1) of the Control of Obscene and Indecent Articles Ordinance.
405. For further information on this Practice Statement, *see* www.hkispa.org.hk/Obscene_e.htm.
406. *See* further Arts 9 and 10 of the Practice Statement; *see also* C. Wright, et al., *Internet Law in Hong Kong* 410 (Sweet & Maxwell 2003).

§2. SEDITION

421. It is an obvious offence if someone commits an act with a seditious intention, which includes an intention to induce hatred or contempt for the government. Under the Basic Law, the government is required to make laws to prohibit any act of treason, secession, sedition or subversion against the Central People's Government of the PRC. This is the famous issue of legislation of Article 23 of the Basic Law. It is currently under heated discussion.

422. The Crimes Ordinance defines the term seditious publication and seditious words as a publication having a seditious intention and words having a seditious intention respectively. Furthermore, the term seditious intention is defined as intention:

(a) to cause hatred or contempt or to excite disaffection against the Government of the PRC or the Government of Hong Kong or the administration of justice in Hong Kong; or
(b) to incite persons to violence; or
(c) to raise discontent or disaffection among the inhabitants of Hong Kong; or
(d) to promote feelings of ill will and enmity between different classes of the population of Hong Kong.[407]

423. The acts of dealing with a seditious publication are conceptually different in nature from the crime of incitement. Offences targeting publications, when the persons involved may not have the intention to incite offences against the state, are a direct restriction of freedom of expression and should, therefore, be narrowly defined in order to comply with the necessity and proportionality criteria as required under the International Covenant on Civil and Political Rights.

424. The objective territoriality and protective principles shall apply to the offence of sedition: the HKSAR shall have jurisdiction over offences of sedition committed by an HKSAR permanent resident anywhere. In the case of other persons, the HKSAR shall have jurisdiction over extraterritorial conduct only if it is intended or likely to incite the offence of treason, secession or subversion or incite violence or public disorder in the HKSAR or has a 'link' with the HKSAR of the kind set out in the Criminal Jurisdiction Ordinance (Cap. 461).[408,409]

---

407. Section 9 of the Crimes Ordinance.
408. The Criminal Jurisdiction Ordinance provides that the HKSAR courts have jurisdiction over offences included in the Ordinance in the following cases: (a) if any of the conduct (including an omission) or part of the results that are required to be proved for conviction of the offence takes place in the HKSAR; or (b) if there has been an attempt to commit the offence in the HKSAR, whether or not the attempt was made in the HKSAR or elsewhere and irrespective of whether it had an effect in the HKSAR; or (c) if there has been an attempt or incitement in the HKSAR to commit the offence elsewhere; or (d) if there has been a conspiracy to commit in the HKSAR the offence wherever the conspiracy is formed and whether or not anything is done in the HKSAR to

425. According to the Criminal Ordinance, it is also an offence to print, publish, sell, offer for sale, distribute, display or reproduce any seditious publication.[410] Based on the analysis above, the offence of sedition can cover websites based on a server in Hong Kong that contain seditious materials. Thus, operators of websites should be scrupulous as to possible seditious content on their sites.

§3. Sex Discrimination

426. Discrimination against women[411] and men[412] is not allowed. This is clearly stated in the Sex Discrimination Ordinance (Cap. 480). This ordinance also prohibits discrimination against people with any marital status[413] and pregnant women[414] in the employment field. Section 43 has some reference to the present discussion. It provides that it is unlawful to publish or cause to be published an advertisement which indicates, or might reasonably be understood as indicating, an intention by a person to do any act which is or might be unlawful by virtue of Part III (on sex discrimination and sexual harassment in the employment field) or Part IV (on sex discrimination and sexual harassment in other fields such as education, provision of goods and services, application for membership to a club, etc.).[415]

427. Thus, if a person distributes any advertisement containing sexual discrimination over the Internet, he or she will be liable according to this ordinance. He or she can establish a defence if he or she can prove: (a) that the advertisement was published in reliance on a statement made to him or her by the person who caused it to be published to the effect that, by reason of the operation of section 43(2),[416] the publication would not be unlawful; and (b) that it was reasonable for him or her to rely on the statement.[417]

§4. Disability Discrimination

428. Disability discrimination is illegal in Hong Kong and is regulated by the Disability Discrimination Ordinance (Cap. 487). It is unlawful to publish or cause

---

further or advance the conspiracy; or (e) if there has been a conspiracy in the HKSAR to do elsewhere that which if done in the HKSAR would constitute the offence, provided that the intended conduct was an offence in the jurisdiction where the object was intended to be carried out.

409. *See* further Proposals to Implement Art. 23 of the Basic Law, Consultation Document, Security Bureau, September 2002, at 25–27.

410. Section 10(1)(c) of the Crimes Ordinance.

411. Section 5 of the Sex Discrimination Ordinance.

412. Section 6 of the Sex Discrimination Ordinance.

413. Section 7 of the Sex Discrimination Ordinance.

414. Section 8 of the Sex Discrimination Ordinance.

415. Section 43(1) of the Sex Discrimination Ordinance.

416. Section 43(2) states that s. 43(1) shall not apply to an advertisement if the intended act would not in fact be unlawful.

417. Section 43(4) of the Sex Discrimination Ordinance.

to be published an advertisement which indicates, or might reasonably be understood as indicating, an intention by a person to do any act which is or might be unlawful by virtue of Part III (on discrimination and harassment in relation to disability in the employment field) or Part IV (on discrimination and harassment in relation to a disability in other fields such as education, provision of goods and services, application for membership to a club, etc.).[418]

429. Furthermore, it is unlawful for a person, by any activity in public, to incite hatred towards, serious contempt for or severe ridicule of another person with a disability or members of a class of persons with a disability.[419] If the vilification involves threats of physical harm, a heavier penalty shall be applied.[420]

430. The phrase 'activity in public' shall include:

(a) any form of communication to the public, including speaking, writing, printing, displaying notices, broadcasting, screening and playing of tapes or other recorded material;
(b) any conduct (not being a form of communication referred to in paragraph (a)) observable by the public, including actions and gestures and the wearing or display of clothing, signs, flags, emblems and insignia;
(c) the distribution or dissemination of any matter to the public.[421]

431. Thus, if a person distributes an advertisement containing disability discrimination or statements involving vilification through the Internet, he or she will be liable. The defence available to him or her includes:

(a) that the advertisement was published in reliance on a statement made to him or her by the person who caused it to be published to the effect that, by reason of the operation of subsection (2),[422] the publication would not be unlawful; and
(b) that it was reasonable for him or her to rely on the statement.[423]

§5. Family Status Discrimination

432. It is unlawful to publish or cause to be published an advertisement which indicates, or might reasonably be understood as indicating, an intention by a person to do any act which is or might be unlawful by virtue of Part III (about discrimination in relation to family status in the employment field) or Part IV (about discrimination in relation to family status in other fields such as education, provision

418. Section 43(1) of the Disability Discrimination Ordinance.
419. Section 46(1) of the Disability Discrimination Ordinance.
420. Section 47(3) of the Disability Discrimination Ordinance.
421. Section 46(3) of the Disability Discrimination Ordinance.
422. Section 43(2) provides that s. 43(1) shall not apply to an advertisement if the intended act would not in fact be unlawful.
423. Section 43(3) of the Disability Discrimination Ordinance.

of goods and services, application for membership to a club, etc.).[424] This has been clearly regulated in the Family Status Discrimination Ordinance (Cap. 527).

433. Accordingly, if a person distributes advertisements that contain discrimination in relation to family status through the Internet, he or she will be liable. The defence available includes proving:

(a) that the advertisement was published in reliance on a statement made to him or her by the person who caused it to be published to the effect that, by reason of the operation of subsection (2),[425] the publication would not be unlawful; and
(b) that it was reasonable for him or her to rely on the statement.[426]

§6. Race Discrimination

434. It is unlawful to publish or cause to be published an advertisement which indicates, or might reasonably be understood as indicating, an intention by a person to do any act which is or might be unlawful by virtue of Part III (about discrimination in relation to race in the employment field) or Part IV (about discrimination in relation to family status in other fields such as education, provision of goods and services, application for membership to a club, etc.).[427] This has been clearly regulated in the Race Discrimination Ordinance (Cap. 602).

435. Accordingly, if a person distributes advertisements that contain discrimination in relation to race through the Internet, he or she will be liable. The defence available includes proving:

(a) that the advertisement was published in reliance on a statement made to him or her by the person who caused it to be published to the effect that, by reason of the operation of subsection (2),[428] the publication would not be unlawful; and
(b) that it was reasonable for him or her to rely on the statement.[429]

436. Furthermore, it is unlawful for a person, by any activity in public, to incite hatred towards, serious contempt for, or severe ridicule of, another person or members of a class of persons on the ground of race.[430] If the vilification involves threats of physical harm, a heavier penalty shall be applied.[431]

---

424. Section 31(1) of the Family Status Discrimination Ordinance.
425. This subsection provides that s. 31(1) shall not apply to an advertisement if the intended act would not in fact be unlawful.
426. Section 31(4) of the Family Status Discrimination Ordinance.
427. Section 42(1) of the Race Discrimination Ordinance.
428. This subsection provides that s. 42(1) shall not apply to an advertisement if the intended act would not in fact be unlawful.
429. Section 42(4) of the Race Discrimination Ordinance.
430. Section 45(1) of the Race Discrimination Ordinance.
431. Section 46(1) of the Race Discrimination Ordinance.

437. The phrase 'activity in public' shall include:

(a) any form of communication to the public, including speaking, writing, printing, displaying notices, broadcasting, screening and playing of tapes or other recorded material;
(b) any conduct (not being a form of communication referred to in paragraph (a)) observable by the public, including actions and gestures and the wearing or display of clothing, signs, flags, emblems and insignia;
(c) the distribution or dissemination of any matter to the public.[432]

§7. Internet Gambling

438. Gambling and lotteries are prohibited in Hong Kong; the same is true regarding promotion and advertising of unlawful lotteries. Thus, there are practices of taking a ship to the high sea to hold gambling sessions. Gambling and lotteries are regulated by the Gambling Ordinance (Cap. 148) in Hong Kong. The term 'gambling' is defined to include gaming, betting and bookmaking. 'Gaming' is further defined to cover games such as chess.[433]

439. The term 'lottery' includes any competition for money or other property success which:

– involves guessing or estimating the results of future events or of past events, the results of which are not generally known; or
– does not depend to a substantial degree upon the exercise of skill by the competitors; and any game, method, device or scheme for distributing or allotting prizes by lot or chance, whether promoted, conducted or managed in or outside Hong Kong;
– however, 'Archbold Hong Kong 2014' questioned the extraterritorial effect of the Gambling Ordinance (Cap. 148) in Hong Kong since no such effect of the legislature is conferred by the Basic Law.[434] And 'Cyberlaw in Hong Kong 2014'[435] confirmed that such extraterritorial effect of section 7(1A) is supported by section 8 with the stipulation of 'whether the bet is received within or outside Hong Kong'.[436]

440. A person who promotes, organizes, conducts, manages or otherwise has control of an unlawful lottery commits an offence.[437] An ISP acting as a host to an online gambling entity shall be possibly considered as assisting with the operation, management and control of a place where bookmaking or betting is promoted or

432. Section 45(4) of the Race Discrimination Ordinance.
433. *R. v. Chen Ta-hoi* [1986] HKLR 1189.
434. K. Bokhary, M. Blanchflower. & I. Cross. *Archbold Hong Kong: Criminal law, Pleading, Evidence and Practice* paras 38–61 (Sweet & Maxwell 2013).
435. P. Stephenson, A. Kwan, & D. Smith, *Cyberlaw in Hong Kong* 196 (LexisNexis 2014).
436. Section 8, Gambling Ordinance (Cap. 148).
437. Section 9, Gambling Ordinance (Cap. 148).

facilitated and is thus likely to be committing an offence. However, a gambling website can be reached worldwide. The general attitude is that promotion in the Hong Kong Press of a gambling website based on a server outside Hong Kong or from a website based on a server in Hong Kong may constitute an offence, but the mere fact of the existence of a website based on a server outside Hong Kong does not constitute such an offence. For example, the promotion or facilitation of bookmaking or betting with a bookmaker is prohibited; however, the prohibition does not apply where the bet can only be placed or is placed by a person outside Hong Kong.[438]

§8. Criminal Liability for Infringement of Copyright and Other Intellectual Property Rights

441. Piracy is very prevalent in Hong Kong. The enforcement of copyright faces an unprecedented challenge. In recent years, the HKSAR Government has been very responsive to industry concerns over piracy. The Copyright Ordinance provides the basic legislation for combating piracy.

442. A person commits an offence if he or she, without the licence of the copyright owner: makes for sale or hire; imports into or exports from Hong Kong otherwise than for his or her private and domestic use; sells, lets for hire or offers or exposes for sale or hire for the purpose of or in the course of any trade or business; exhibits in public or distributes for the purpose of or in the course of any trade or business which consists of dealing in infringing copies; possesses with a view to its being sold or let for hire by any person for the purpose of or in the course of any trade or business or its being exhibited in public or distributed by any person for the purpose of or in the course of any trade or business which consists of dealing in infringing copies; or distributes to such an extent as to prejudicially affect the owner of the copyright an infringing copy of a copyright work.[439]

443. A person can also be criminally liable if he or she makes, imports into or exports from Hong Kong, possesses or sells or lets for hire or offers or exposes for sale or hire an article specifically designed or adapted for making copies of a particular copyright work which article is used or intended to be used to make infringing copies of the copyrighted work for sale or hire or for use for the purpose of or in the course of any trade or business.[440]

444. According to the ordinance, those who indulge in copyright piracy, production of infringing articles on a commercial scale or possession of infringing articles for trade or business can be liable to a maximum fine of HKD 50,000 (USD 6,140) per infringing article and a term of imprisonment of up to four years. Import or export of pirated articles is a criminal offence. It is also an offence to be involved

---

438. *See* further s. 16B, Gambling Ordinance (Cap. 148).
439. Section 118(1) of the Copyright Ordinance.
440. Section 118(4) of the Copyright Ordinance.

in copyright piracy outside Hong Kong for the purpose of importation into Hong Kong. Sanctions are also available against those who manufacture and sell technology for defeating technological copyright protection systems.

445. Furthermore, considering the fact that much-pirated material is produced near the border in China, Hong Kong should also enact the broadest possible offence of 'accessory' to copyright piracy, thus enabling prosecution of those who use Hong Kong as a base to direct piratical operations outside the territory.[441]

446. The Customs and Excise Department is responsible for enforcing the criminal aspects of infringement of intellectual property rights. It investigates complaints alleging infringement of trademarks and copyright and complaints alleging false trade descriptions. The department has extensive powers of search and seizure and cooperates with overseas enforcement authorities and owners of trademarks and copyright in a concerted effort to combat infringement of intellectual property rights. The department has received many commendations for its work from both public and private institutions.

§9. Interception of Communications

447. Privacy is highly respected in Hong Kong. It is stated in the Hong Kong Bill of Rights Ordinance that no one shall be subjected to arbitrary or unlawful interference with his privacy, family, home or correspondence, nor to unlawful attacks on his or her honour and reputation.[442] Similar rules are also provided in the Basic Law:

The freedom and privacy of communication of Hong Kong residents shall be protected by law. No department or individual may, on any grounds, infringe upon the freedom and privacy of communication of residents except that the relevant authorities may inspect communication in accordance with legal procedures to meet the needs of public security or of investigation into criminal offences.[443]

448. The Interception of Communications and Surveillance Ordinance (Cap. 589) came into force on 9 August 2006.[444] The aim of the ordinance is to provide a tool for 'preventing or detecting serious crime'[445] or 'protecting public security'.[446] Section 4(1) provides that no public officer shall, directly or indirectly (whether through any other person or otherwise), carry out any interception.

449. However, the ordinance provides several exceptions:

441. Excerpt from the IIPA Special 301 Recommendations, 20 Feb. 1996 (available at www.iipa.com).
442. Article 14(1) of Hong Kong Bill of Rights Ordinance.
443. Article 30 of Basic Law.
444. It revokes and replaces the Interception of Communications Ordinance (Cap. 532) which never came into force. P. Stephenson, et al., *Cyberlaw in Hong Kong* 142 (2d ed. Lexis Nexis 2007).
445. Section 3(1)(a)(i) of the Interception of Communications and Surveillance Ordinance.
446. Section 3(1)(a)(ii) of the Interception of Communications and Surveillance Ordinance.

(a) any interception carried out pursuant to a prescribed authorization;
(b) any interception of telecommunications transmitted by radio communications (other than the radio communications part of a telecommunications network for the provision of a public telecommunications service by any carrier licensee under the Telecommunications Ordinance (Cap. 106)); and
(c) any interception authorized, permitted or required to be carried out by or under any enactment other than this ordinance (including any interception carried out in the course of the execution of an order of a court authorizing the search of any premises or the seizure of any evidence).[447]

450. Section 5(1) provides that no public officer shall, directly or indirectly (whether through any other person or otherwise), carry out any covert surveillance. Exception applies to any covert surveillance carried out pursuant to a prescribed authorization.[448]

451. Surveillance is categorized into Type 1 surveillance and Type 2 surveillance. The latter category is broad enough to cover all types of 'listening to, monitoring or recording words spoken or activity carried out by any person' whether with or without the consent of that person.[449] Type 1 surveillance is any covert surveillance other than Type 2 surveillance. In addition, a Type 2 surveillance is regarded as Type 1 surveillance if it is likely that any information which may be subject to legal professional privilege will be obtained by carrying it out.

452. There are several factors to take into consideration when deciding whether to authorize an interception or surveillance under this ordinance. Section 3(1)(c) imposes a proportionality requirement. The relevant factors in determining whether the proportionality test is satisfied are:

(a) the immediacy and gravity of:
    (i) where the purpose sought to be furthered by carrying out the interception or covert surveillance concerned is that of preventing or detecting serious crime, the particular serious crime to be prevented or detected; or
    (ii) where the purpose sought to be furthered by carrying out the interception or covert surveillance concerned is that of protecting public security, the particular threat to public security.
(b) the likely value and relevance, in relation to the purpose sought to be furthered by carrying out the interception or covert surveillance, of the information likely to be obtained by carrying it out.[450]

453. There are three categories of authorization – judge's authorization, executive authorization and emergency authorization.[451] An application for a judge's

447. Section 4(2) of the Interception of Communications and Surveillance Ordinance.
448. Section 5(2) of the Interception of Communications and Surveillance Ordinance.
449. Section 2(1) of the Interception of Communications and Surveillance Ordinance.
450. Section 3(2) of the Interception of Communications and Surveillance Ordinance.
451. Section 2(1) of the Interception of Communications and Surveillance Ordinance.

authorization can be made in writing supported by an affidavit to a panel judge for any interception or Type 1 surveillance.[452] An application for an executive authorization can be made in writing to an authorizing officer for Type 2 surveillance.[453] An application for an emergency application can be made in writing to a head of department if it is considered that there is an immediate need for the interception or Type 1 surveillance to be carried out by reason of an imminent risk of death or serious bodily harm of any person, substantial damage to property, serious threat to public security or loss of vital evidence and having regard to all circumstances of the case that it is not reasonably practicable to apply for the issue of a judge's authorization.[454] The departments authorized to make an application are the Customs and Excise Department, Hong Kong Police Force, ICAC and Immigration Department.[455]

§10. Offences Concerning Personal Data

454. Personal Data is regulated by the Personal Data Privacy Ordinance. Detailed rules have been provided to procure the legitimate use of personal data. This ordinance further provides several actions which could constitute offences.[456] The basic standard in defining the liability relies on whether the person intentionally supplies any information which is false or misleading in a particular way and which is so supplied for the purpose of having the data user concerned comply with relevant requests or causes psychological harm to the data subject through unconsented disclosure.[457]

§11. Telecommunications Offences (Transmission of Information)

455. The Telecommunications Ordinance contains criminal provisions. This is very important to the safe transmission of information through the telecommunications infrastructures. The ordinance has contemplated two types of persons who might commit the offences. A telecommunications officer or whoever had official duties in connection with a telecommunications service shall be guilty if he or she:

– wilfully destroys, secretes or alters any message that he or she has received for transmission or delivery;
– forges any message or utters any message that he or she knows to be false or altered;

452. Section 8 of the Interception of Communications and Surveillance Ordinance.
453. Section 14 of the Interception of Communications and Surveillance Ordinance.
454. Section 20 of the Interception of Communications and Surveillance Ordinance.
455. Schedule 1 of the Interception of Communications and Surveillance Ordinance.
456. For example, s. 35E(4) provides the situation of a data user using personal data in direct marketing without data subject's consent; s. 35L(7) provide the situation when a person fails to comply with a written notification from a data user to cease to use personal data in direct marketing.
457. *See* further s. 64 of the Personal Data (Privacy) Ordinance.

- wilfully refrains from transmitting any message or wilfully intercepts or detains or delays any message;
- in pursuance of his or her duty or as directed by a court, copies any message or discloses any message or the purport of any message to any person other than the person to whom the message is addressed.[458]

456. All other persons who are outside the scope of section 24 shall be guilty if they wilfully secrete, detain or delay a message intended for delivery to some other persons; or having been required by a telecommunication officer to deliver to him or her a message for delivery to some other persons, refuses or neglects to do so.[459]

457. Section 27A of the ordinance is much more meaningful in the present sense. It regulates the activities of obtaining unauthorized access to any program or data held in a computer through telecommunications. This provision is consistent with the Crimes Ordinance in prohibiting access to a computer with criminal or dishonest intent.[460] This constitutes the so-called computer hacking. According to this provision, computer hacking is a criminal offence liable on conviction to a fine of HKD 20,000. To constitute a crime, the person must have performed the activity knowingly with the intention of obtaining unauthorized access.[461]

458. The ordinance also holds criminally liable the action of damaging, removing or interfering with a telecommunications installation with intent to prevent or obstruct the transmission or delivery of a message or intercept or discover the contents of a message. The person committing this offence shall be liable on summary conviction to a fine at level 4 and to imprisonment for two years.[462]

459. Transmitting or causing to be transmitted by telecommunications a false distress, urgency, safety or identification signal shall be an offence if the person knows or believes it to be false or has the intent to deceive. This offence shall be liable for summary conviction to a fine at level three and to imprisonment for two years.[463]

---

458. Section 24 of the Telecommunications Ordinance (Cap. 106).
459. Section 25 of the Telecommunications Ordinance (Cap. 106).
460. Section 161 of the Crimes Ordinance.
461. Section 27A of the Telecommunications Ordinance.
462. Section 27 of the Telecommunications Ordinance.
463. Section 28 of the Telecommunications Ordinance.

Chapter 3. Application of Criminal Procedural Law in the Area of ICT

460. Generally speaking, legislation is only concerned with conduct taking place within the territory for which it is legislated. However, there are exceptions which are expressly provided in legislation. For example, certain offences relating to lotteries will apply if the promotion, selling, buying and publication take place in Hong Kong, even if the relevant lottery is promoted, conducted or managed outside Hong Kong. The Criminal Jurisdiction Ordinance (Cap. 461) also provides that in relation to certain theft and forgery offences, any question as to where the relevant event occurred should be ignored.[464]

461. The Criminal Jurisdiction Ordinance also provides the location of events for jurisdictional purposes as long as the property was obtained in Hong Kong, the property is either dispatched from or received in Hong Kong or when there is a communication in Hong Kong of any information, instruction, request, demand or other matter if it is sent by any means from Hong Kong to elsewhere or from elsewhere to Hong Kong.[465]

462. In the area of ICT, when the server and the operator are located within Hong Kong, there shall be no problem about jurisdiction. However, the story is different once the server and the operator are both located outside Hong Kong. Since criminal law is territorial in nature, the court in Hong Kong shall enjoy no jurisdiction in such cases.

463. With the development of e-commerce, businesses can easily cross national borders entirely through software and Internet agents rather than through physical existence or human agents. Domestic regulation on activities like banking, stock brokering and gambling will be increasingly ineffective. Thus, it is necessary to make modifications concerning criminal jurisdiction.

464. Does computer-generated evidence or e-evidence have the same validity as traditional evidence? Section 9 of the ETO (Cap. 553) reads: 'without prejudice to any rules of evidence, an electronic record shall not be denied admissibility in evidence in any legal proceeding on the sole ground that it is an electronic record'. Thus, its validity is recognized. However, we should note that section 13(1) of the ordinance states that section 5 (requirement for writing), section 6 (digital signature), section 7 (retention of information in original form) or section 8 (retention of information) does not apply in relation to information given, presented or retained or signatures required for the purposes of any proceedings set out in Schedule 2 (relates to proceedings before all the courts and most tribunals in Hong Kong), unless any rule of law relating to those proceedings provides for its application.

---

464. Section 3 of the Criminal Jurisdiction Ordinance.
465. Section 5 of the Criminal Jurisdiction Ordinance.

465. Nevertheless, section 13 further specifies that it shall not affect any rule of law permitting the use of electronic records or electronic signatures. The requirements in section 13(1) only apply to procedural issues. For a complete understanding, reference should be made to the Evidence Ordinance (Cap. 8).

466. Section 22A of the Evidence Ordinance acknowledges that a statement contained in a document produced by a computer shall be admitted in any criminal proceedings as prima facie evidence of any fact stated therein if:

(a) direct oral evidence of that fact would be admissible in those proceedings; and
(b) it is shown that the conditions in subsection (2) are satisfied in relation to the statement and computer in question.[466]

467. This section further defines the conditions referred to in subsection (1)(b):

(a) that the computer was used to store, process or retrieve information for the purposes of any activities carried on by anybody or any individual;
(b) that the information contained in the statement reproduces or is derived from information supplied to the computer in the course of those activities; and
(c) that while the computer was so used in the course of those activities:
    (i) appropriate measures were in force for preventing unauthorized interference with the computer; and
    (ii) the computer was operating properly or, if not, that any respect in which it was not operating properly was not such as to affect the production of the document or the accuracy of its contents.[467]

468. Additional requirements are set out in section 22A(3) that a statement contained in a document produced by a computer used over any period to store, process or retrieve information for the purposes of any activities ('the relevant activities') carried on over that period shall be admitted in any criminal proceedings as prima facie evidence of any fact stated therein if:

(a) direct oral evidence of that fact would be admissible in those proceedings;
(b) it is shown that no person (other than a person charged with an offence to which such statement relates) who occupied a responsible position during that period in relation to the operation of the computer or the management of the relevant activities:
    (i) can be found; or
    (ii) if such a person is found, is willing and able to give evidence relating to the operation of the computer during that period.
(c) the document was so produced under the direction of a person having practical knowledge of and experience in the use of computers as a means of storing, processing or retrieving information; and

466. Section 22A(1) of the Evidence Ordinance.
467. Section 22A(2) of the Evidence Ordinance.

(d) at the time that the document was so produced, the computer was operating properly or, if not, any respect in which it was not operating properly or was out of operation was not such as to affect the production of the document or the accuracy of its contents, but a statement contained in any such document which is tendered in evidence in criminal proceedings by or on behalf of any person charged with an offence to which such statement relates shall not be admissible under this subsection if that person occupied a responsible position during that period in relation to the operation of the computer or the management of the relevant activities.

469. When electronic records are used in evidence merely to prove a fact, but not the truth of their contents, they are not subject to the requirements of section 22A. However, even if section 22A does not apply, a court will still need to consider section 22B.[468] Section 22B(3) deals with the weight to be given to the evidence above. The court shall draw reasonable inference from the circumstances, especially whether or not the information is supplied contemporaneously with the occurrence or existence of the facts in question and whether or not any person concerned with the supply of information or the operation of the computer has any incentive to conceal or misrepresent the facts.[469] Thus, several elements shall be relevant in deciding the weight of the electronic evidence: the nature of the contracting process; the security of the storage and retrieval system and the method of authentication used by the parties.

468. *Secretary for Justice v. Lui Kin Hong* [2000] 1 HKLRD 92.
469. Section 22B(3)(b) of the Evidence Ordinance.

Chapter 4. Conclusions

470. In this information age, the HKSAR has endeavoured to lead the way forward. It has already put in the pipeline the necessary legal framework for e-commerce. No doubt a law-abiding society and self-disciplined population will reduce the costs to the society and therefore enhance its competitiveness. Ordinances have been made or modified to meet the demands of e-commerce; however, a constant review of the adequacy of the regulatory environment is important to the constantly changing information society.

471. Considering its persistently advocated policy of full competition in Hong Kong, various interest groups have been taking up an important position in formulating guidance or rules for transactions over the Internet and exerting influence on governmental policies and ordinances. This has been evidenced by the analysis of various topics in this monograph.

472. For the time being, e-commerce in Hong Kong is still experiencing dramatic increases both in complexity and in competitiveness. Cyber law provides the tools for promoting the further development of e-commerce. In fact, so-called cyber law does not exist with specific rules. It is dispersed in separate statutes and ordinances. This situation, in turn, creates difficulties in obtaining an overview of the laws regulating e-commerce at first glance. Furthermore, with further development of e-commerce, more rules or regulations shall be modified or added to complement the framework for the regulation of e-commerce. It is this steady and relentless development that makes a complete monograph describing cyber law in specific regions necessary.

473. The descriptions in this monograph shall contribute to a common base of knowledge and to the creation of a viable framework in terms of issues to be confronted and concepts for carrying out e-commerce in Hong Kong. Fortunately, the legal ideology in Hong Kong does provide for a framework of communication and interaction that allows information and knowledge to flow freely among all social groups and consequently constitutes a very good social basis for setting out the appropriate legal structure to deal with specific issues.

474. No doubt, cyber law in Hong Kong shall continue to develop, or more exactly, the HKSAR shall further legislate or modify more statutes and ordinances to accommodate further development of e-commerce in Hong Kong and to live up to its ideal to be an IT hub. It is expected that constant review and update of rules for e-commerce shall be vital to obtaining the right attitude and understanding of the policies in Hong Kong.

Selected Bibliography

Abbott, F.M. & D.J. Gerber (eds). *Public Policy and Global Technological Integration*. Kluwer Law International, 1997.

Altes, W.F.K. et al. (eds). *Information Law Towards the 21st Century*. Kluwer Law International, 1992.

Banisar, D. & S. Davies. 'Global Trends in Privacy Protection: An International Survey of Privacy, Data Protection, and Surveillance Laws and Developments'. *John Marshall Journal of Computer & Information Law* 18 (Fall 1999): 49.

Berthold, M. & R. Wacks. *Data Privacy Law in Hong Kong*. FT Law & Tax, 1997.

Centre for Asian Business Cases. *Building Electronic Commerce Infrastructure: The Hong Kong Retail Sector (A)*. The University of Hong Kong, 1999.

Centre for Asian Business Cases. *Fighting 21st Century Pirates: The Business Software Alliance in Hong Kong*. The University of Hong Kong, 1999.

Chong, R.B. & W. Chow. 'Financing Telecommunications Projects in Asia: A Promising Regulatory Perspective'. *Federal Communications Law Journal* 52 (December 1999): 9–11.

Diederiks-Verschoor, I.H.Ph. *An Introduction to Space Law*. 3rd ed. Kluwer Law International, 2008.

Dobinson, I. & D. Roebuck. *Introduction to Law in the Hong Kong SAR*. Sweet & Maxwell, 1996.

Grewlich, K.W. *Governance in 'Cyberspace': Access and Public Interest in Global Communications*. Kluwer Law International, 1999.

Mueller, M. *Telecom Policy and Digital Convergence: The Hong Kong Economic Policy Studies Series*. City University of Hong Kong Press, 1997.

Narayan, A. & L.K. Thakur. *Internet Marketing E-commerce and Cyber Laws*. Authorpress, 2000.

Ruiz, B.R. *Privacy in Telecommunications: A European and an American Approach*. Kluwer Law International, 1997.

Rustad, M. & C. Daftary. *E-Business Legal Handbook*. Aspen Law & Business, 2001.

Scherer, J. (ed.). *Telecommunications Laws in Europe*. 3rd ed. Kluwer Law International, 1995.

Smits, J.M. *Legal Aspects of Implementing International Telecommunication Links: Institutions, Regulations and Instruments*. Martinus Nijhoff Publishers, 1991.

Srivastava, D.K. (ed.). *Business Law in Hong Kong*. 2nd ed. Sweet & Maxwell Asia, 2007.

Selected Bibliography

Stephenson, P., A. Kwan & D. Ellis. *Cyberlaw in Hong Kong*. 2nd ed. Lexis Nexis, 2007.

Warren, S.D. & L.D. Brandeis. 'The Right to Privacy'. *Harvard Law Review* 4 (1890): 193.

Wesley-Smith, P. *An Introduction to the Hong Kong Legal System*. 3rd ed. Hong Kong: Oxford University Press, 1998.

Wright, C., W. McAuliffe & A. Gamvros. *Internet Law in Hong Kong*. Hong Kong: Sweet & Maxwell Asia, 2003.

Wu, R. 'Electronic Transactions Ordinance-Building a Legal Framework for E-commerce in Hong Kong'. *Journal of International Logistics and Trade* 1 (2000).

Zhao, Y. 'The Commercial Use of Telecommunications under the Framework of GATS'. *Air & Space Law* 24 (1999): 304–328.

Zhao, Y. 'A Dispute Resolution Mechanism for Cybersquatting'. *The Journal of World Intellectual Property* 3 (2000): 849–865.

Zhao, Y. 'Internet Service Providers and Their Liability'. *Law/Technology. World Jurist Association* 34 (2001): 1–19.

Index

The numbers here refer to paragraph numbers.

3G, 14, 73, 74

Abusive practice, 214
Acceptance, 129, 229, 248, 262–266, 338, 373
Access, 17, 18, 20–23, 30, 35, 36, 39, 43, 52, 58, 68, 74, 82, 89, 140, 154, 156, 220, 223, 240, 244, 245, 318, 323, 350–351, 361–362, 373–374, 376, 386–387, 393–394, 403–404, 410, 415, 457
Addressee, 267–270
Administrative proceeding, 111
Admissibility, 259, 283, 464
Affidavit, 256, 453
Agency, 103, 267, 334
Alternative dispute resolution, 105–107
Anti-competition, 77
Applicable law, 235, 278, 279, 280, 349
Application service provider (ASP), 24
Appointment, 40, 129
Arbitration
  general, 107, 110, 115, 119–120, 122, 123–131, 132
  panel, 128
Arbitrator, 120, 125–130
Asian Domain Name Dispute Resolution Centre (ADNDRC)
  domain name dispute supplemental rules, 109
  general, 108–110
Assessment, 253, 323–326, 333, 376
Assessor, 130, 326
Audit, 33, 166, 225, 294, 318, 340
Authentication, 33, 89–90, 95, 286, 287, 318, 469
Availability, 125, 210, 311, 339, 392

Back-up copy, 163, 221
Bad faith, 115–116, 214, 215
Bargaining position, 339
Basic Law, 8, 10, 399, 421, 439, 447
Basic telecommunications, 68
Bilingual, 39, 103
Bona fide, 117, 209
Business efficacy, 159, 271
Business registration certificate, 205, 208, 210, 248
Business-to-business (B2B), 29
Business-to-consumer (B2C), 28
Business-to-government (B2G), 246

Cable programme, 134–135, 138, 146, 148, 153, 344
Carrier licence, 63, 66
Cause of action, 337
Certification authority (CA), 125, 255, 281, 290, 293–295, 297–306
China Internet Network Information Centre, 110
Chinese mark, 179
  practice statement, 294, 298, 302, 305, 308–309, 359, 363, 420
  requirement, 100
Class licence, 63, 66
Classification, 84, 96, 97, 417
Clicktrail, 394
Clickwrap, 272
Closest relationship, 270
Code of
  conduct, 382
  practice, 244, 294–295, 298, 305, 348–349, 359, 362, 382, 401
Commercial
  entity, 205
  exploitation, 168–169

Index

Commissioner of Customs and Excise, 102, 159–160, 334, 446, 453
Competition
  general, 17, 19, 55–56, 58, 69, 73, 76–78, 80–85, 88, 166, 439, 471
  policy advisory group (COMPAG), 80
Competitor, 5, 116, 166, 178, 182, 439
Complaint, 112–113, 119, 123, 349, 380–381, 395–397, 407, 446
Complainant, 115–116, 122, 381
Computer
  chip, 168
  crime, 403–407
  programme, 134, 135, 138, 146, 148, 153, 245, 267
Conduct regulation, 84
Confidential information, 203, 337
Confidentiality, 125, 287, 325
Confusion, 116, 155, 178, 180
Consideration, 116, 262, 452
Consultancy, 225, 242
Consultation paper, 351
Consumer
  bill of rights, 332, 447
  choice, 19
  confidence, 293, 331
  contract, 277, 280, 334
  council, 333, 401
  goods, 274, 334, 364–366, 368
Content owner, 217, 369–370
Contingency plan, 318
Copyright
  general, 133–156, 159–161, 163–165, 167, 182, 217–218, 220–223, 282, 343–344, 350, 352, 417, 441–446
  infringement, 159, 182, 343
Cost-effective, 26, 132
Counterclaim, 129
Country of origin, 200
Court order, 196, 256
Cross-referencing, 304
Cross-subsidization, 83
Cryptography, 91, 94, 250
Cryptosystem, 288, 292
Custom and Excise Department, 230
Cyberport, 48–51
Cybersquatting, 214

Data
  protection, 373, 375, 390
  subject, 373–374, 386, 388, 389, 390, 391, 395, 454
  user, 373, 378–380, 383–387, 390–391, 395, 454
  user return, 383–384
Database, 89, 165–167, 318, 362, 384
Decency, 413, 414, 416
Decode, 91
Defamation, 354–357
Defective goods, 274, 344, 364
Depravity, 414
Deregistration, 209
Derogatory treatment, 141, 143, 144
Design, 33, 42, 141, 173, 183, 192–194, 205, 225–227, 242, 325, 416
Determination, 126, 298
'Digital 21', 45–51, 281
Digital
  certificate, 33, 294, 304, 307, 308
  signature, 92, 95, 250, 253, 255, 281, 283–292, 301–305, 464
Diligence, 273, 336, 390
Dilution, 178, 180
Direct
  infringer, 189, 191
  marketing, 391–392
Disability discrimination, 428–431
Discount, 33, 86
Discovery, 185
Discretion, 120, 126, 397
Dispute
  general, 105–112, 114–119, 124–126, 129, 131, 132, 215, 235
  resolution, 105–112, 114–119, 124, 125, 215
  resolution mechanism, 105, 125
  resolution provider, 107, 110, 118
Distinctiveness, 173
Distortion, 143
Distributed approach, 83
Distribution, 23, 156, 230–235, 274, 430, 437
Documents only arbitration, 126
Documentary proof, 210–211
Domestic regulation, 463
Dominant licensee, 64, 86
Domain name
  general, 107–119, 123, 182, 197–215
  registration agreement, 114, 120
Duty of care, 337, 341

E-Cert system, 300, 307–309
Electronic
  banking, 310–328

communication, 43, 255
contract, 254, 259–260, 262–270, 272
data, interchange (EDI), 26, 29, 33, 87, 246
information, 256
payment, 327–328
record, 250, 253, 255, 257, 259, 261, 265–269, 283, 285–288, 291, 464–465, 469
service delivery (ESD), 38–40, 103
signature, 284–291, 465
E-government, 35–53
Electronic Transaction Arbitration Rules, 124–131
Embezzlement, 403
Emergency
general, 227, 238–239, 453
service, 239
E-money, 32
Encode, 91, 250
Encryption
general, 90–91, 93–95, 166, 232, 318, 394
symmetrical key, 91
Enforceability, 266, 318
Entry restriction, 84
Espionage, 403
Evidence, 115–117, 126, 199, 205, 259, 283, 406, 449, 453, 464–466, 468–469, 471
Exchange rate, 313–314
Exclusive
jurisdiction, 413
licence, 62–63, 66, 73, 149
right, 138, 146, 150, 174, 182, 194
Exemption clause, 244, 254, 274–275, 280, 338
Expedited procedure, 126
Export, 1, 3, 6, 25, 33, 35, 79, 94–96, 99–101, 147, 159, 181, 219, 230–231, 276, 442–444
Express term, 222, 271
External telecommunications facility, 17, 72, 73
Extortion, 403

Facilities management, 241–243
Fair use, 117
False attribution, 141, 145, 155
Family status discrimination, 432–433
Fee, 62–63, 122, 128, 211, 213, 223, 225, 239, 378, 380, 383, 422
Feedback, 225, 378
Fine, 367, 379, 419, 444, 457–459
Firewall, 318, 325
Fit and proper person, 295–296
Foreign ownership, 54
Forgery, 403, 460
Formality examination, 187, 193
Fraud, 318, 403–404
Freedom, 399, 423, 447

Gambling, 438–440, 463
Gazette, 161, 248–250, 291, 377
Generic item, 256
Globalization, 81
Government-to-business (G2B), 38
Government-to-citizen (G2C), 38
Government Office Automation (GOA), 43
Government Supplies Department (GSD), 247–248
Grace period, 235
Guidelines to assist the interpretation and application of the competition provisions, 85

Hacking, 404, 457
Hardware
general, 216–218, 238, 241, 403
contract, 216–218
manufacturer, 217
supplier, 216
Hearing, 111, 120, 126, 130
Hong Kong Article Numbering Association (HKANA), 33
Hong Kong Consumer Council, 333
Hong Kong Domain Name Registration Company Ltd. (HKDNR), 110, 114–118, 202, 204, 208, 210–211, 213
Hong Kong International Arbitration Centre (HKIAC), 107–110, 112, 125, 127–129, 215
Hong Kong Internet Registration Corporation Limited (HKIRC), 201–203, 215
Hong Kong Internet Service Providers Association (HKISPA), 21, 244, 348, 359, 362–363, 420
Hong Kong Monetary Authority (HKMA), 229, 312–314, 316–317, 319–320, 321, 323, 326, 328
Hong Kong Network Information Centre, 201

Hong Kong Post, 299–300, 304, 306, 307
Hong Kong Productivity Council, 219
Hong Kong Quality Assurance Agency, 103
Hong Kong Society of Accountants (HKSA), 124–125
Hyperlink, 153, 154, 155, 182

Impartiality, 120
Implied
  licence, 159
  term, 236, 244, 271–273
Import
  declaration, 230
  general, 3, 79, 94–96, 99, 147, 149, 159, 169, 181, 190, 194, 230–232, 276, 358, 419, 442–444
  licence, 99, 232
Importation right, 139
Imprisonment, 94, 367, 379, 419, 444, 458–459
Incidental copy, 146, 154, 352
Indecency, 413–414
Indecent article, 358–363, 368, 411, 416
Indecent material, 351, 353, 359, 362, 420
Independence, 120
Independent Commission Against Corruption (ICAC), 400–401, 453
Indirect infringer, 191
Information Infrastructure Advisory Committee (IIAC), 41, 45
  security, 166, 318
  system, 257–258, 267–269
  Technology and Broadcasting Bureau (ITBB), 41, 45
  Technology Services Department (ITSD), 42
Innocent
  defence, 358
  publication, 356
Inspection, 235, 239, 385
Installation, 18, 242, 245, 458
Integrity
  general, 42, 93, 125, 245, 259, 287, 313, 325
  right, 141, 144
Intention, 116, 146–147, 209, 214, 262, 271, 284, 289, 354, 394, 398, 404, 421–423, 426, 428, 432, 434, 454, 457
Interception, 448–453
Interconnection
  general, 58, 60, 64, 74, 82, 170
  charge, 82
Interference, 7, 64, 78, 447, 467
Intermediary, 269
Internet banking, 31–32, 203, 229
Internet content provider (ICP), 350
Internet Corporation for Assigned Names and Numbers (ICANN), 108–109, 111, 114, 123, 198, 202, 215
Internet protocol (IP), 197
Internet service provider (ISP), 17, 21, 208, 213, 348–363, 394
International
  direct dialling (IDD), 73
  International marketing supervision network (IMSN), 333
  Standard Organization (ISO), 103–104, 250
  Telecommunications Union (ITU), 15, 75
Investigation, 318, 381, 397, 399, 406–407, 447
Investment, 6, 7, 17, 74, 79, 83, 88, 178, 233, 314
Invitation to open tender, 248

Joint Universities Computer Centre (JUCC), 201
Jurisdiction, 123, 209, 277, 278, 413, 460–463

Lawful use, 163, 221
Layout-design, 168, 170–172, 193
Legislative council, 9, 40, 82, 251, 283, 347
Legitimate use, 391, 454
Level playing field, 7, 54, 78
Libel, 354
Liberalization, 17, 19, 67–75, 81
Licence, 23, 35, 38, 59–60, 62–66, 70, 73, 74, 85–86, 86–88, 94, 96, 97, 99, 147, 148–150, 154, 159–160, 167, 189, 222–223, 231, 232, 344, 442
Licensee, 59–60, 64, 72–73, 85, 90, 160–161, 449
Licensing
  condition, 77
  of strategic commodities information sheet, 98
  regime, 59, 159–160, 163, 167
Liquidation, 296
Literary work, 134, 136, 165, 220
Litigation, 105, 123
Lottery, 439–440, 460

Mailbox rule, 264–265, 268
Maintenance contract, 236–240
  Back-up copy, 163, 221
Mandatory arbitration proceeding, 115
Market
  force, 45, 79
  share, 219, 320
Matching procedure, 388–392
Merchantability, 272
Merchantable quality, 334
Minimalist regulatory approach, 252
Misappropriation, 166, 404
Misuse, 408, 409
Mobile
  communication, 14
  telecommunications, 73
Model law, 283
Monetary policy, 313–314
Money laundering, 403
Monopoly
  franchise agreement, 61
  general, 81–82
Moral right, 141–145
Morality, 416
Mutilation, 143
Multi-class application, 176
Mutual
  jurisdiction, 123
  recognition, 102, 304

National Arbitration Forum, 124
Negligence, 274, 336–342
Negligent misstatement, 341–342
Network
  operator, 17, 73, 74, 87, 343–346
  security, 325
  service, 14, 244–245
Non-competition, 166
Non-disclosure, 166
Non-profit, 107, 198, 201, 205, 213
Non-obviousness, 183
Non-profit organization, 107
Non-repudiation, 125, 287
Novelty, 183

Objection, 177, 351
Objective cost-based approach, 82
Obscene
  article, 358–363, 411–414, 416
  Articles Tribunal (OAT), 413, 418
  material, 351, 359, 362
Obscenity, 413–414

Offer
  general, 11, 26, 28, 70, 86, 101–102, 107, 117, 136, 169, 176, 181, 185, 188–190, 193–194, 239, 240, 248, 262–264, 266–268, 307, 317, 342, 348, 410, 425, 442–443
  of amends, 354–355
Office of the Telecommunications Authority (OFTA), 19, 56–57, 66, 82, 244, 401
Omission, 122, 336
Online application form, 208
Online registration process, 210
Operational standard, 198
Ordinary care, 336
Originality, 150, 152, 154, 220
Originator, 267–270, 352
Outsourcing, 320

Panellist, 120–122
Parallel importation, 139
Patent, 183–191
Patentability, 185–186
Paternity right, 141
Penalty, 379, 429, 436
Personal data, 328, 332, 371–397, 400, 402, 454
Personal identification number (PIN), 351
Physical
  facility, 343, 352–353
  signature, 282
Piracy, 158–160, 167, 223, 235, 441, 444–445
Place of business, 270
Pornography, 403
Pre-classification, 96–97
Primacy, 123
Primary infringement, 146–147
Priority, 187
Privacy, 125, 328, 349, 371–403, 447, 454
Privacy Commissioner for Personal Data, 377–382, 396, 401
Private key, 92, 288, 292, 308
Procurement, 37, 225, 228, 249–247
Product
  liability, 364–370
  safety, 100
  standards, 100, 101
  standards information bureau (PSIB), 100–101
Proof of intention, 146
Property right, 95, 134, 159, 168, 183, 209, 218, 229, 235, 404, 441–446

Index

Proprietor, 189–191
Propriety, 416
Public key
  general, 91, 92, 250, 288, 288, 292–293, 301–302, 308
  infrastructure (PKI), 91, 292
Public
  order, 423
  service, 38–39, 281
Publicity, 398
Purchasing power, 314
Pure economic loss, 341

Quasi-regulatory power, 353

Reasonable
  care, 273, 334, 337, 356–357
  opportunity, 334, 347, 358
  time, 273, 334
Reasonableness, 275, 338–339
Receipt rule, 264–265, 268
Recognized certificate, 287, 290, 297, 302, 305
Resource allocation, 84
Registration
  document, 205
  fee, 211, 213
  general, 38, 84, 114, 116, 174, 177, 179, 193, 197–215, 230, 248, 393
Rejection, 334
Remote monitoring, 240
Repository, 305
Reproduction, 140, 150, 154
Repulsiveness, 414
Reputation, 33, 143, 175, 214, 319, 447
Response, 113, 119–120, 128, 227, 240, 245, 316, 406
Revenue generation, 84
Review, 80, 99, 119, 213, 470, 474
Rights management information, 218
Royalty, 62, 171
Rule(s) of law, 235, 256, 259, 275, 286, 464–465

Secession, 421, 424
Second-level domain (SLD), 200, 202
Secondary infringement, 147
Security
  general, 28, 42, 89, 125, 127, 166, 242, 251–253, 287, 294–295, 308, 316, 318–319, 323–326, 340, 376, 399, 402, 447, 448, 469
  bureau, 406
  management, 89
Sedition, 421, 424, 425
Seditious intention, 421–422
Self-governance, 13, 307
Sensitivity, 96, 373, 375
Service classification, 84
Service mark, 115–117, 209
Sexual discrimination, 427
Slander, 354
Small and medium-sized enterprise (SME), 24, 26
Smart card, 32, 311, 327
Software
  general, 95, 157–159, 163, 183, 219–224, 226, 232, 235, 238, 241, 243, 272, 346, 463
  contract, 219–223
  development service, 224, 226
  vendor, 219
Spectrum, 56, 57, 73–74
Standardization, 103, 242
Standards and calibration laboratory (SCL), 102
Statement of
  claim, 129
  defence, 129
  reply, 129
Statement on competition policy, 77–78, 80
Strategic commodity, 94, 96–99, 231
Statutory declaration, 256, 295, 298
Subsidiary legislation, 256
Subversion, 421, 424
Summary conviction, 458, 459
Supply chain management, 24, 29, 246
Symmetric algorithm, 94
System engineering service, 228

Tariff, 64, 79, 86
Taxation, 84
Technology crime division, 407
Telecommunications
  authority (TA), 19, 56, 58, 60, 399
  carrier, 343
  infrastructure, 13, 455
  installation, 458
  officer, 455
  system, 148, 344
Tender, 37, 247–248, 468
Terrorism, 403
Theft, 403–405, 460

Third-party dispute resolution, 124
Timeline, 128, 235
Top-level domain (TLD), 107–108, 110, 200, 201
Topography, 168, 170, 172, 193
Trade and industry department, 96–98, 231
Trade description, 181, 195–196, 334, 446
Tradelink, 33, 35, 116, 303
Trademark
  general, 115–117, 173–182, 196, 199, 209, 214, 215, 446
  infringement, 180, 214
Trade secret, 166, 195–196
Traffic engineering service, 224, 227
Training, 51, 224, 226, 241, 245, 276
Treason, 421, 424
Tripartite relationship, 202
Trust
  general, 252–253, 256, 293
  mark scheme, 333
Turnkey, 224, 229

Unauthorized access, 89, 318, 394, 403–404, 457
Unconscionable contract, 236, 280, 334
Uniform Domain Name Dispute Resolution Policy (UDRP), 109
Uniform Domain Name Dispute Resolution Policy Rules, 109
Unilateral, 120
United Nations Commission on International Trade Law (UNCITRAL), 283
Universal service, 64, 83
User-friendly interface, 224
Utility, 183, 246

Valid presence, 207
Validity, 62–63, 188, 244, 260–261, 266, 275, 282, 285, 287, 290, 293, 302–303, 464
Value-added service, 87
Video link, 126
Violence, 414, 422, 424
Virtual bank, 319–322

Warning, 361–362, 366, 394, 411, 418, 420
Warrant, 209, 225–226, 256, 272–273
Warranty, 225–226, 370
WebTrust, 124–125
Weights and measures, 102, 334
Wills, 256
Wireless Local Area Networks (WLAN), 23, 245
World Intellectual Property Organization (WIPO), 133
Writing, 121, 136, 220, 259–260, 261, 283, 291, 386, 390, 430, 438, 453, 464

www.ingramcontent.com/pod-product-compliance
Ingram Content Group UK Ltd.
Pitfield, Milton Keynes, MK11 3LW, UK
UKHW021239300926
15471UKWH00013B/701

9 789403 522760